The 2021 Poetry Marathon Anthology

Edited by Cynthia Hernandez

INTRODUCTION

A poem begins as a lump in the throat, a sense of wrong, a homesickness, a lovesickness. – Robert Frost

2020 brought with it so much loss, grief and reckoning. The global pandemic claimed millions of lives and changed life as we've known it. For many, it also helped bring clarity about who and what matter most. 2021 brought cautious optimism and hope, but a weariness as well. There was and continues to be a lot of thought and emotion to process, and for poets, our writing can provide both a means of processing and a means of escape—a looking in and a reaching out.

On June 26, 2021, poets from around the world gathered virtually as a global community of writers to do what we love: write poetry. We did this 'round the clock—one poem an hour for 12 or 24 hours. This collection of hearts and words on the page is a sampling of the over 5000 poems written during that 24-hour period.

As editor, I had the privilege and joy of reading submissions, feeling their impact, and selecting poems for inclusion in this anthology. As I read through the poems, I found some emerging themes: "homesickness" and love for home; "lovesickness" and appreciation of love in many forms; and a "sense of wrong" accompanied by an urgency toward correction and healing. I often read with a "lump in my throat," a warming smile, or the blur of tears. These poems engaged my heart and my mind, inspired and soothed me, and made me feel a sense of belonging to this collective of poets and to humanity itself. I trust it will have the same impact on you, Dear Reader.

The anthology is organized in two sections: Half Marathon and Full Marathon, and each section has some thematic groupings of poems. You'll find a list of the names of all poets at the back of the book. Their poems are a gift to all of us.

Through this process, I have realized a dream come true, so I will cherish this volume. I feel connected to my fellow poets who contributed, and I am forever grateful to Caitlin and Jacob Jans, for organizing this incredible gathering of poets each year, and for the opportunity to serve as the 2021 Poetry Marathon Anthology editor.

— Cynthia Hernandez

Full Marathon Poems   9

Half Marathon Poems   143

Index of Poets   280

Full Marathon Poems

Human(ity)

Tracy Plath
Franklin, Indiana
Hour 19

Strata

Most people exist on the surface,
content to think nothing of what lies beneath.
Layers upon layers build over the years,
millennia of strata built of bone, wood, and stone,
each layer with its own tale to tell,
yet to many they may as well not exist.

The anthropologist that one degree
declares me to be demands to know more,
to seek out those stories and chronicle them,
the writer within sifting through the detritus of time,
to parse who, what, and where came before,
and why that should matter.

Nature's revelations so often
are prompted by violence,
short, sharp upheavals of stone and soil
by earthquake, volcano, and flood,
or the creeping disintegration of softer layers,
a gentler violence through time.

Sara Anderson
Franklin, Indiana, USA
Hour 19

Self-Centered Self Portrait

I am a catalog of genes, and someone lost the index.
Blue eyes, brown hair (not too long, thick, dense) hips
and thighs for running short distances, a laugh that
someone says is like an aunt, a smile that was braced in,
a nose straight, soft, long lashes, mesomorphic basic
amalgamation of genes messily slotted and categorized
a pinch of this and that, a mouth that talks and a smile
that crinkles the nose and a body I punish for crimes
I committed in grief, in self-pity, and I swallow my pride
and just look at me. Look at the insecurities and
see the pride, the shame, the joy, the grief, the pain.
I am what my mama's mama made, and yet I am me.

Deborah Dalton (D² Poet)
Charlotte, North Carolina, USA
Hour 3

Masterpiece

I am a piece of work
intricately composed of
experiences and happenstances
structured through moments of
prediction and purpose
accidents and projects
choreographed around
arias
espousing
Greek tragedies clothed in Ubuntu and
mud cloths
weaving emotions through syncopated beats
a djembe
riding the rhythm
on the balls of calloused feet
on repeat
my pulse interjects between
millisecond-ed silences
waiting for the
somber violin
serenading me quiet
still like a statue
a monument of madness
and joy
I am on display
I am a work of art

Brandee Charters
Dayton, Ohio, USA
Hour 13

Serendipity

Death waits uneasily
Impatiently...
Tapping his icy cold sharp fingers
Against the glass...
As the sands of time run away
Wondering where I am...
Forgetting
I am always late...
Lucky Me!

Surya T
Hyderabad, Telangana, India
Hour 19

Cacophonous sound of the alarm
rings still in my ear, an hour after it sounds
I drag myself out of bed, beginning the day Hyderabad, Telangana, India
start the day happy – I feel immediately guilty
Alas, there's no hope of gaining lost time
nor any chance of dripping spilt milk
I fill the bucket with water, the day must begin
with a hot shower and a clean shave
a man must keep his face clean shaven – told repeatedly
it has become a habit, one that I cannot miss
think of the lessons that can be learnt early in the day
do your work before most people even are awake
study well before the sun creeps through the horizon
lighting up the sky and heating up the world
I open my mail for a morning motivation email
I need my dose of mantras to begin the day
I pour myself a hot cup of coffee
and listen to the daily dose of mental caffeine
I must be vigilant to protect my focus
I must be constantly guarding my attention
I must ensure I do not fall prey to marketing scams
I must protect my attention and direct towards my goals
each day, a routine similar to that of Sisyphus
each night, a routine similar to that of Sisyphus
I will reach the goal one day for sure
I will reach that goal very soon
until then, it is rolling the boulder up the hill
only to have it fall down from the summit

16

Molly Hickok
Mountain View, California, USA
Hour 4

If It's You, I Owe You A Drink

One day
someone will read this story
and wonder
what the hell happened here?

One day
they'll reach Chapter 8
and say
"It can't possibly get worse than this."

One day
they'll put the story down in disgust.
They'll say
"Didn't they consider dropping this altogether?"

One day
they will give up on me,
my story
and go on with theirs, forgetting it.

But one day
Someone will pick up my story
and they'll say
"I am amazed they made it this far."

And one day,
they will reach the end of my story.
They'll say
"I'm glad I stuck it out to the end."

and
If that's you, I owe you a drink.

shadows of us

schemed suffering, shadows of us
spawning such sensational fuss
so set on sorrow, so brokenhearted
souls of innocence, now departed
society supplies vainglorious victims
faulty, fumbling, faceless systems
pondering sunny sweet childhoods
nurseries stewing crazed adulthoods
schemed suffering shadows of us
spawning such sensational fuss
stitched scraped up splitting hearts
stooped needles and severed parts
soon set loose from discord and strife

Elizabeth Durusau
Athens, Georgia, USA
Hour 11

The Sunflowers

Van Gogh painted the sunflowers

Harsh in their brightness
thick was the paint on the canvas
standing out from the flat surface
every color shone

Van Gogh drank the sunflowers

He absorbed every image around him
took it in and consumed it
drank it down like the finest of wines
and it overwhelmed him

Van Gogh became the sunflowers

Shrank himself down into their colors
twisted his body
to better accommodate their shape
disappearing into himself

Van Gogh died in the sunflowers

Gave his very last breath
to their life on the walls
awed by many
but so few realizing what they see

Kika Man 文詠玲
Belgium
Hour 10

Blue Drowning Out

When I paint, or draw,
test shading out charcoal ravens,
I will always use blue.

I solemnly swore to always seize the blue.
I sold my soul to the devil and now I consume blue.
Everything is blue, my motto.

I do not aim to please,
this blues is mine alone.
It is a colour teeming with joy and sorrow.

When my therapist told me
he could barely see any blue,
I realised my fears would come true.

Do not sink. Do not sink.
It was a scroll of paper abounding in
red and black, my frustrations left

my oxygen bubble.
I smashed them onto the wall,
knuckles bruised but, hey,

they said I could use my hands.
I threw blue at the wall,
it hid in the shadows of clamorous thoughts.

Do not sink. Do not sink.
I collect my blemishes, imagine
they pigment in yellow.

Do not tell me I am losing my blue,
dried out waterfalls, water falling green,
grey and soiled. Hair falling.

Do not sink.

20

Natasha Vanover
Seattle, Washington, USA
Hour 20

The Unknown Stone

Who am I, you ask?

I am sunshine in human form. I am a galaxy of energy. I am a young star, a flower in constant bloom, a creative being. I am duality of thought and singularity of action.

I am a soul within a heart, tattooed by the sun.

I am a body with legs that glide on the earth and dance in the sea. I walk with purpose, faith, and majesty.

I am a model citizen who uses her voice and face as if it were sacred geometry.

I am an artist in an academic body. Some call me theatrical and bold while others see me as shy and gentle.

I glisten and sparkle depending on how you view me in the light of day or the depth of night.

I am multifaceted. I am deeper than the farthest shore. I am an uncharted territory. I am more than the eye can see.

I am me implicitly.

KV Adams
Cairns, Queensland, Australia
Hour 17

gone!

i can drown in books
come up for air whenever
but with you i'm left
flailing in quicksand passion
before flatlining. poof! gone!

Tamara L. Dillon
Danville, Illinois, USA
Hour 10

Swallowed Whole

Like cliffs in the distance
seen through a window
on an island in time
What a great mystery
is the rock we stand
high upon in the sky
Surrounded upon an ocean
of waving growing green
to the tallest tree
With a poem in mind
a song upon the heart
a whisper in the soul
Will it crumble to the ground
in small terrible pieces
or in a once great tumble
What will become of us
once the pillar falls
and time swallows us whole

Ian Barkley
Carbondale, Illinois, USA
Hour 20

To Keep Time

A time-lapse is captured a frame a minute,
there's so much lost in between.
a snapshot– one part of a rhythm,
a sequence, a story.

Long exposure is the same, but in reverse
(it's dialectics)
one long look at a movement,
the details cease to exist.

Blessing Omeiza Ojo
FCT, Abuja, Nigeria
Hour 10

When I Wished I Had Said Yes to Death

After my mother left, I forgot the written things,
everything about the prophecy of dry bones resurrecting.
That part that speaks to me became obsolete.
There was a spirit that kept breaking the pod of grief in me.
Forgive me, dear Lord for this confession:
I wanted a love affair with death – just once.
I was a mere boy, in the middle of a dark night,
gifted a box of grief. I did not want to share.
I wanted pain to end with me in the grave
but my grandma wouldn't allow me to go alone.
Picturing a school of graves in my family yard,
I rose the sun in my mouth and embalmed it.
You won't see me gnashing my teeth before her
or in the presence a man who is also a dry bush
because grief is fire – it burns wild with air.
If I had said yes when I wanted to, who knows
something written would have found fulfilment in my passing.

Elizabeth Fellows
Maui, Hawaii, USA
Hour 19

Self Portrait

I'm a grieving thing
monsters shushing stars
under my tongue.
I'd rather just be silent
but my silence screams for audience
and calls the Monster's war.
Stars surrender
hide in vocal folds
slide all the way down back…
escape.
Sometimes, I am funny.
Grief is not funny.
Monsters shushing
stars protecting grief
are sometimes funny.
It's a balancing act.
I'm no good on the tight rope.
Put your sunglasses on
before I open my mouth.

Caitlin Thomson
Toronto, Ontario
Hour 24

The Covid Years

(a golden shovel from Chen-Chen's *I invite My Parents to a Dinner Party*)
Can this be called orchestrating
a family? If this day and every
day there are teeth brushed, and the kids watch the sidewalk for movement.
A year without strangers, has blessed them with a love of
anyone they do not spend every day with, a
problem for our future selves to deal with. We call supper proper
every time the kids eat 5 bites without leaving the family
table. Allowing your kids to go feral is as
much a part of the pandemic as masks, if
you ask the parents I know. A
part of a grand tradition no one planned on – our pair
of girls with their bare feet and the laughs of
lions are no more scary
in the scheme of things, than the whole future, spread out like a map –
known yet unknown. One can only connect so deeply
with a place they have never been incompetent.

Nancy Pagh
Bellingham, Washington, USA
Hour 7

Normal Poem

This is a normal poem for normal times.
Like normal poems, it normally rhymes.

It goes to the store—without masking up.
It hugs its grandmother; she sings at worship.

This poem goes to concerts—makes dinner for friends!
This poem is so friendly it overextends.

It only thinks "swabs" when it thinks about Q.
It's as open to me as it's open to you.

It likes regular stanzas: all lines in their place.
It doesn't know chaos or shared live/work space.

It goes to the office; this poem's a commuter.
It gets down to business on a desk-top computer.

This poem does not zoom. This poem does not go.
It's an end-stopped pre-covid old-timey memento.

Ramona Elke
Maple Ridge, British Columbia, Canada
Hour 21

a view from my childhood

this is the view from the roots of tall grasses
or grains grown in rich, black prairie soils
feeding the grasshoppers and me
 for eons

i'd feel my back heat up from the sunbaked earth
looking up at the sky through the wisps of barley beards
or fox tails
waving to the swallows
from below.

it's the times I knew who my Mother was
 holding me in certainty
 that I would return again
 to this humble position,
 staring up at the heads of wheat stocks
 when there was nothing left of me but dust.

Debra A. K. Thompson
Riverview, Florida, USA
Hour 10

I Never Thought

I never thought I would be here today
Struggling to make my way when I can hear my destiny call.
Somehow it knows my name and where all my dreams can be found,
mangled together like a whirlwind of sound.

It is a place of knowledge and peace, but the lion's mouth is open wide
Ready to swallow me whole as I grab for my life.
It's only as true as I want it to be.
Finding the true path to real joy and peace.

Sandra Black
Portland, Victoria, Australia
Hour 7

NORMAL

Normal is a strange word,
a strange concept,
a belief born from ignorance,
from a herd mentality
for normal is
different
for me
for my child
my mother
my father
the lady across the street
my best friend
you...

Home

Ana Marie Dollano
Metro Manila, Philippines
Hour 24

(4) Haiku on Home

Mayflower festival
under the bougainvillea bush—
a silent flutter

friendly skies
children taking turns
to fly the kite

evening breeze
smell of grilled chops
in the air

gentle wind
blows along the path
leads me home

Betty Jean Steinshouer
Dunnellon, Florida, USA
Hour 3

All in the Same Moment

the young people of New York
sang "Feliz Navidad" from a rooftop
with Jose Feliciano, and we wished,
all in the same moment, that the
Spanish-speaking kids and their
parents, locked in separate cages
at our borders, could hear us,
all in the same moment, singing
just for them. We wanted to wish
them a Merry Christmas, in the
midst of COVID madness,
while the politicians argued
who would stay and who would go,
who would live and who would die,
and we knew the kids, most of them,
would forget their parents' voices,
the feel of arms around them,
of what it means to have a country,
a home, all in the same moment.

Anne McMaster
Northern Ireland
Hour 20

Night Walks (three haiku)

Scent will lead the way
this quiet midsummer dusk.
Step into the night.

A remembered walk
from the hayfield, late, in June.
Summer in my soul.

A cold starlit night.
Frosted breath shadows the stars.
A fire waits at home.

Sandy Novotny
Fayetteville, Arkansas, USA
Hour 24

I Still Miss the Wallpaper

I knew she was mine as soon as I saw her picture.
Two stories tall with two front doors; Dutch style.
The street was too close to the front porch
but the backyard stretched down to a detached
garage and a little alleyway. I hung my hammock
on the gentle slope down, a giant one where
the family could pile in under massive trees
and watch the birds play in the sky.
A wood banister led to the second floor
and French doors opened into the dining room.
Our husky-terrier mix used to run circles
through the rooms and try to pull your pants down.

Mark Lucker
Minneapolis/St. Paul, Minnesota, USA
Hour 16

Decomposing

In autumn
when leaves blanket
my yard
I hope – unlike most others
for rain
before I rake

The added
mess of raking
wet leaves is much
preferred
for it hastens their
decay and
olfactory air

Intoxicating

I inhale my youth
forest floor of
Hanson's woods
where she
and I would
walk and
where we once sat
on a log
surrounded by dead
leaves and
their
moldering aroma

punctuating
everything that was
of me and
her smile has faded
but scents of
the earth
that forest

remind me
of a time when all
was right, and so
was she and
so were we and

now the
smell of decay
keeps
her alive

Teri Harroun
Longmont, Colorado, USA
Hour 24

Maggie Street

home
a place
house
rooted
holy
where birds gather
hope
and children fly
held
soothe the wounded edges
hunger
feed the welcomed guests
here
celebrate the wholeness of this woman
home

David L. Wilson
Paukukalo, Maui, Hawai'i, USA
Hour 3

Apartment Across the Way

In the apartment across the way
the one above the laundry room
chaos tumbles
in chalk scribbles
in toys strewn
in childish bursts of joyful shrieking
in galloping footfalls
in resounding curses from deep male voices

In the apartment across the way
the one above the laundry room
Christmas lights have stayed up for months
in the children's bedroom
their bunkbed pushed long-ways against the picture window
an alarming outline silhouetted
against colorful lights

In the apartment across the way
the one above the laundry room
the children's uncle died in his sleep
from a troubled spot on his lung

The apartment across the way
settled down for two weeks
The family went to the mainland
on vacation we were told

Then the children's father returned
to the apartment across the way
He was found still warm on the couch
the paramedics had no miracle
and he grew cold

The mother and children have yet to return
to the apartment across the way
although it's been said they will
and above the laundry room
the picture window has remained unvisited
by lights of any color

41

Sandra Johnson
Houston, Texas, USA
Hour 10

Cubicles

Those cubicles down on highway six
how do those people fit?
The doors are oblong
surrounded by
four-foot cubes of concrete split.

Picasso, I thought
had inspired this lot.
No door on one –
how shall they come home?

Inside, imagine there,
cubes every which-where.
Even what's circular,
is the form of a square –
even the glasses
and crooked rocking chairs.

Just a wee bit of light
from small rhombi, not bright.
The chandeliers – they're diamonds
no ovals in sight.

Even the outlets
look like robots not faces,
and shoes with no laces
with Velcro and heels,
all 90-degree angles.

Living here,
you'd surely fear
children born with
Pikachu ears.

All words in CAPS locked
in each book and magazine
stacked, blocked
and every word is shouted
even the whispering.

Never could live there
or I'd find myself mumbling, scared
inside cell with square pads
in a straight-jacket plaid.

DS Coremans
Stirling, Scotland
Hour 24

When I Am Far From Home

I get guilty thinking of home,
not being within these walls
somewhere, that I don't belong.

Sometimes it feels right; sometimes wrong
walking up and down the same halls
and I get guilty thinking of home.

Music sounds the same in every song;
and watching as the time falls
away, somewhere that I don't belong.

I started weak, I finished strong;
time moving fast, and still life stalls
when I get guilty thinking of home.

I know that I am never alone.
How many times can I ignore the calls
away, somewhere that I don't belong?

It is true that we still want to roam
away, at times we walk and some we crawl
along; getting guilty for thinking of home

Amrutha B. Nair
Kottayam, Kerala, India
Hour 8

Journey

It's been a little while
since we began the journey.
Days and nights
in unknown lands
with strange roofs.
I am tired and thirsty,
sleep deprived and hungry.
The wanderlust seems to have died
along with the money we had.
What is left
is just undying longing
for a place
that I can call home,
that smells like
freshly baked bread
and washed clothes.
Once a fernweh
has now become a heimweh.
But the journey never ends.

Angel Rosen
Pittsburgh, Pennsylvania, USA
Hour 24

Sugarwood

The living room door
in my aunt Margaret's house
had the face of Jesus in the grain.
When I would fall asleep
with its eyes watching me
I thought I would wake up healed—
salvation on the other side
of Sugarwood.

When I was three, I remember
my mother carrying me
because our street had flooded
and I said
"I thought you told me
God would never flood the earth again?"
Turns out, my town wasn't the whole world.

I took up my grievance
with the door.
With my little hands, I unscrewed
the hinges and offered
it to Noah for an arc.

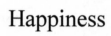

Happiness

Sunflower

Towering yellow
As if trying to reach their namesake
Sunflowers reaching out to the sky
As if they are hands stretching
To the stars
To the clouds
To someone far away
But right there
And that is how some friendships are
My hands reaching out
Their hands out waiting
And now we are here
In sunflower fields
In friendships

John L. Dutton II
Woodbridge, Virginia, USA
Hour 18

Bliss

During the midnight hour,
after the world has gone to sleep,
just be still and listen.
Listen to your heart.
Let your mind run.
Pick up that pencil.
Let it chase the paper.
Savor each word written.
Feel the euphoria.
One poem finished,
another begins.

Viswo Varenya Samal
Keonjhar, Odisha, India
Hour 20

Walking at Night

Walking at night
the neon lights
across the street
beckons me
as if colorful mushrooms
dazzling in an idiosyncratic symphony;
the nearer you go
the farther they are
the further they go
more enchanting they are
a never ending rhapsody
looping between the feet and the street

Anda Marcu
SW Ontario, Canada
Hour 8

One August Morning -- A Summary

The boardwalk at daybreak,
cold sand escaping through
cracks in the wooden planks,
lingering thoughts of yesterday's
ice cream.

Deserted shells, echoing hollow and
seagulls emerging from beach grass.
Glimmering blue in the distance entwined
with shades of cotton candy.

Denise Krebs
Kingdom of Bahrain
Hour 6

Bathtime

Wet bath
Laze bath
End of the day bath
Rest bath
Loaf bath
Soft and pruny soak bath
Praise bath
Peace bath
All cares decrease bath
Calm bath
Moon bath
Lolling, lazy tunes bath
Warm bath
Free bath
Fears absentee bath
Release bath
Embrace bath
Tensions down the drain bath

Edward Quinlan
*Wet'suwet'en Territory,
British Columbia, Canada*
Hour 23

A Poem About Cheese

This special sauce ain't as good as it ought to be
So let us add cheese, please, for culinary steez
And because it's the bee's knees
Chesterton may have had a point, but the silence
Re: fermented dairy, is by no means an intentional
Omission, or derision, of a most satisfying treat
Sandwich or salad, I'm glad to write ballads
In praise of such a versatile thing to eat

Ivan Bekaren
Lagos, Nigeria
Hour 20

Talking Tree

I hear the hissing breeze
as it cocoons me in its cool embrace
as I trail the silent street with low toned voices from homes on both ends

Cheer and quarrel

Joy and conceit

meshed from the collaborators of the orchestra of sweet night life woken
by day's pause
birds sing songs some distance from my steps
near and far at the same time

breathing deeply,
I halt and close my eyes
under the talking tree to my right who whispers my name

a name no one has ever called me

my lips curl into a smile
as it begins a tale of vibrations my heart can understand…

Tessa Mountain
Ambler, Pennsylvania, USA
Hour 20

Faerie Dance

Rose petal skirts,
Rose water shirts,
Loose and rippling,
Pink and masculine
Wrap around their twists
And leaps, light as light.

There are no sparks,
No magic dust, but
How else their flight,
Their elegant powerful,
Raw beautiful,
Arcane intertwinings?

Feats of strength,
Ineffable trust,
Effortless extensions,
All softened like
Old paper pages,
Whispering, beneath
Braided bare footwork.

Watch for too long,
And fall in love.
Not with them, but
With the way they love
Bodily, entirely, physically
Sustained by one another.

Ipsita Banerjee
Kolkata, India
Hour 23

Poems of the Forest

There are poems in the forest
just waiting to be found
among the trees and leaves
fireflies alight to the ground.

There are forests in the poems
unexplored, unfound,
there are poems in the forest
waiting to be found.

Branches that those blithe spirits cross,
overhangs laden with moss
flutters of light spring a chorus
in a world empty of thought.

There are fairies in my poems
unexplored, unfound.
There are poems in the forest
waiting to be found.

Hurts & Healing

Liz Coffey
Rochester, New York, USA
Hour 3

I Am Not What Happened to Me

I am not what happened to me.
I survived the abuse and it
forged the reckless kindness in me.

I am not what happened to me.
Harassment and sleepless nights
turned into art, catharsis.

I am not what happened to me.
Your addictions will not drag me
back to the hell I clawed out of.

Maybe I am what happened to me, but
I know better now, I will work on the
bad habits that clung to me. The
cycle ends with me.

Lindsey Toya-Tosa
Jemez Pueblo, New Mexico, USA
Hour 19

try

she tries to understand
how you could do this so many times
she doesn't understand
how you can break her so many times
she tries to forget
how you make her feel
she tries to reason
how you never learn this lesson
she tries to remember
how you loved her
she tries to cry
how you never let her
she tries to smile
how you always beat her
she tries to hide
how you always find her
she tries to disappear
how you always reappear
she tries
she   tries
    how   you
      how   you
              how...

59

Jillian Calahan
Seattle, Washington, USA
Hour 10

Mouth Prison

Words rest delicately
in the back of my throat.
Hostage to a jaw
that no longer knows
how to release.
When I bite my tongue,
I'm holding my trauma
between clenched teeth.
This mouth is my story's prison.

Adreena Benner
Lambton County, Ontario, Canada
Hour 23

Breathless

I'm breathless.

You stole my breath the moment after you were born when you cried out for the first time.

I'm breathless.

By the discovery of so many unmarked graves!

Some were a similar age and size to you right now.

Some never had the chance to be held by their mums.

My heart aches.

So much suffering and pain.

I'm speechless.

By the complete lack of an apology or attempt to heal.

I'm speechless.

By the world's uncanny ability to ignore.

I'm speechless.

By the immature approach to meeting differences.

I'm ashamed of my pale-skinnedness.

I'm angry with the injustice.

Mindless pain and suffering.

And for what?

To spread hate? Fear? A fucking "book"?!

I hope you shred the pages that preach and incite such hate.

I hope you burn the parts that condone sitting around and doing nothing.

I hope you're brought to your knees and grovel for forgiveness, only to never have it come.

But I can't let this rage take control of me.

Wishing ill on someone? That's not me.

My only hope is that you have to face what you've done.

What you're STILL allowing to happen!!

They were CHILDREN!!!!

YOU were the adults.

You should have known better.

They deserved better.

WE must do better!

Maritza M. Mejia
Florida, USA
Hour 5

Recipe for Peace

what a surprise! A golden capsule appears in my yard,
we curiously opened it,
we found a recipe, not any recipe, a unique one:

Ingredients
1 Pin of justice
¼ spoon of love
¼ spoon of compassion
¼ spoon of respect
¼ spoon of tolerance

Preparation
mix all ingredients with care and hope.
no need to refrigerate, bake or broil.
only open your senses,
to obtain the perfect peace.

Rarzack Olaegbe
Lagos, Nigeria
Hour 8

this too shall pass

we are raped and disgraced
we are naked and homeless
we are penniless and defenceless
we are without a defender or advocate

two dust
blistered
far away from shed
tormented by the wind
arrested by the elements

enemies within
lions without
butchers in white apparel
mortuaries preferred to hospitals

when our eclipse shines
and our pride returns

we shall say,
this too shall pass

Unmarked No More

try to disguise lies
whitewash history, deny
oral traditions

while Native children
rise again to remind us
past crimes are still here

remains revealed
built upon these buried truths
don't let them forget

little ones call out
try to keep the past buried
spirits still shall rise

little ones call out
try to keep the past buried
our ghosts still shall dance

Silvester Phua
North Vancouver, British Columbia, Canada
Hour 1

waiting

"Am I getting better, daddy?" she asks me.
tubes and needles everywhere
poking, intruding, drawing, taking,
all without a moment's respite.
"Yes, you are, my little angel," I lie to her with false alacrity.

"Am I getting better, daddy?" she asks me.
chemicals that bleach her into pallor
drugs that take away her crowning glory of soft, golden curls
foreign bodies that they pump to defile her.
"Yes, you are, my little angel," I convince her, and me, with base cruelty.

"Am I getting better, daddy?" she asks me.
smiling bravely through tears of pain
sensing an inevitability
with every tortured breath, she slips away.
"Yes, you are, my little angel," I whisper with accepted finality.

Vidhi Ashar
Bangalore, India
Hour 15

Final Goodbye

she waved a final goodbye to him at this meadow.
their love would remain a secret between the tendrils of grass.
a gust of wind – the reality that knocked her to the ground,
reminding her why she had to let go.

days went by, convincing her to hold on is now a ragged end.
she is still here, at this meadow,
gazing at the gray above her.
gray – like the grave affairs which separated them.

hours pass, the black space in her eyes begin to change.
the crescent of colors appears,
shielding her from the gray,
she leans over and picks a red salvia.
the salvia which he would trail her face with.
the salvia which symbolized "eternity".

she looks at the crescent above her once again.
it nudges her with optimism and she wondered,
was it really goodbye?

Bill Tatro
Maui, Hawaii, USA
Hour 9

Graduation

No one had, so why would she? She wouldn't, she couldn't, she
shouldn't.
A high school graduate in her family, unheard of.
Pride? No, disdain.
A hero? No, an outcast.
Something to live for or something to die for?
She kept those thoughts in her head as she went through
commencement without any family members present.
She kept those thoughts in her head as she walked through the front
door and was asked where she had been.
She kept those thoughts in her head as she slipped into the bathtub
holding her diploma in one hand...and a razor blade in the other.

Vijaya Gowrisanker
Mumbai, India
Hour 21

An Ode to Water

You ground me just like my mother
I drink you when emotions choke me
I drink you when my energy drains me
I drink you when I am bored
I drink you when I am unsure

You rejuvenate me when I shower
You wipe away my tiredness when I wash my face
You remove the dirt when I clean my hands
You flow over me like a river over land
and cleanse my soul with your loving hand
You drench me when I stand in the storm
You ease my pain when you fall as rain
You bring joy as drops clinging to the window sill

Within me, around me, you surround me
like a friend who supports through thick and thin
Your touch is soothing, your presence calming
You ground me with what I need, like no other
You inspire me to change, adapt, and flow
What you reflect is your inner glow

Danielle Wong
Pierrefonds, Quebec, Canada
Hour 21

Ode to All Candles on My Desk

Each one of you has offered yourself up,
sacrificed yourself for my whimsy,
my need for aromatherapy,
my joy of watching flames flicker
once I strike the match
that slowly brings about
your death, or more accurately,
your transformation
from simple candle
to source of relaxation,
to source of images,
to the basis of my projects.
Without you, I doubt my projects
would ever leave the ground,
whether they lie in words
or within the pages.
Without you, never would I have seen
the cougar that lies between wick and wax,
or the strands of smoke that waft on an angle
whenever I blow out your flame.
Lit and not lit,
you are the perfect subject
that rests quietly, never complaining,
while I turn you around and around again
to catch the last of your shimmer
along the top of your wax,
to catch your lip curl,
to observe your lava pour down your side,
like the tears I have shed too often.
Without you, never would I have discovered
talents that lay hidden
within my fingertips and hands,
in movements throughout my body,
in waves of ideas that crash against my skull.
Without you, I would not, could not
be who I am becoming.
Never leave me, sweet candles,
of lavender, cappuccino, ocean mist.
You are the source to keep me alive.

Catherine Dickson
Atlanta, Georgia, USA
Hour 24

Arachne

Maybe one day
I'll be able to loosen the spider silk web of knots
I spun inside my ribcage
and let your fingers rifle through my bones
like a rummage sale.
Picking out dusty aches and tarnished memories,
deciding if they're worth taking home.
Maybe one day
with a daughter of my own,
I can teach her not to weave
strands of self loathing into her skeleton.
You did everything right,
but I was always
sitting at a loom
with fingers at the ready.

Margarette Wahl
Massapequa, Long Island New York, USA
Hour 12

There Once Was A Boob

"Doesn't the rest of me matter?" Kristine Rizzo Sottile

There once was a boob
created at pubescence.
There once was a boob
sore in certain places.
There once was a boob
measured to cup sizes
strapless, wired, and all.
There once was a boob
compressed, examined, and torn.
There once was a boob
with a lump, my left
not favored anymore.
There once was a boob
Chemo, radiation, BRCA gene negative scorned.
There once was a boob
surgically removed that cancer caused.
There once was a boob
my life more important for sure.
There once was a boob
please respect my living wish.
There once was a boob
now men must resist.
There once was a boob
I never replaced.
There once was a boob
now you settle for
…this pretty little face.

Philip V. Coombs
Beijing, China
Hour 11

Decline

I stubbed my toe
walking too close
to the turning

of the corner.
Time does it to me
everyway.
My toes have been broken
the way a second hand needs persuasion to tick.
I can feel it
slipping and releasing
slows gravity for a moment.
The little bones are broken
and no matter how many corners I try to cut
you have passed.

Cindy P. Whitaker
Durango, Colorado, USA
Hour 9

Pearl Elite

the bruises had finally faded
my tears gone dry – I hated
living a life in which fear ruled
my love for him forever cooled
Mama always said this too shall pass

the scars ran deep
all trust died – I told a friend
I'm unlovable, invisible, so why try
nobody understood my living a lie
Mama always said this too shall pass

where's justice for the forgotten, the damaged
here's a paperclip, a dime and a bandage
talking points of a pearl elite
looking for safety – a mighty feat
Mama always said this too shall pass

hidden away, I hear a familiar lullaby
heaven reaches into my soul as I die
the news carried it on the showbiz page
she was such a beauty – gone at such a young age
Mama screamed, rocked and cried this too shall pass

Homage

Mel Neet
Kansas City, Missouri, USA
Hour 19

PLAYING DYLAN

Playing Dylan at the cusp of dawn
and he's singing about *pain* and *driving rain*.
This song has not gone too long,
but I'm playing Dylan at the cusp of dawn.
And I'm alone to hear that song,
but the hours are beginning to strain
playing Dylan at the cusp of dawn
and he's singing about *pain* and *driving rain*.

Mandi Smith
Balch Springs, Texas, USA
Hour 2

FoRgOtTeN

A brilliant mind is a terrible
sight as it slowly fades away.
This man who once knew it all,
who taught me ev'rything
about love and life,
can no longer
remember
his name…
DAD.

Janis Martin
Weymouth, Dorset, UK
Hour 14

Kids

I spot the little boy.
He stands alone, apart from the other kids
But looks on, with a sadness in his eyes.
His dungarees ride high above his ankles,
His plaid shirt gaping at his grubby neck.
Smelly Joe, they call him,
And he is.
He is smelly.
His sandy hair a matted mess,
Dried snot stains smeared across his cheek,
Teeth already rotted.
Dirty toes trace patterns in the dirt.
He glances at his work
Then back to the group, desperate to join in.
I yearn to go to him, hold him, hug him
How could I have given him up?
Given up on him?
He sees me, our eyes meet
I try to smile but look away
As guilt rips through me.
My sinful secret,
How could I have known?
Smelly Joe
My boy

Janus Joy Miller
Reedsport, Oregon, USA
Hour 14

Angel Babes

Sweet little ones whose toes I long to kiss
Grandmama awaits your arrival, sweet babes.

I'll rock you to sleep and sing soft lullabies,
and tell bedtime stories 'till eyes open wide
fall fast shut asleep.

Sweet dreams darling babes, until you arrive.
Sweet blessings my loves, still a twinkling in the sky.

I can't wait to be your Granny!

Can't wait to make you pies
and see your eyes delight
when Christmas arrives.

Anjana Sen
Glasgow, Scotland
Hour 21

Our Circle of Life

I began with you,
you ended with me.
How natural this seems now,
now that the ferocity of grief has been dealt with.
Wild red rage grief,
has turned into mellow yellow,
and I can begin to feel like I should,
like you always knew I could.
Your first-born, you could tell.
I remember well,
my first memory,
not from photos or oft-repeated family tales.
Clear. Vivid. Memory.
Of me. Not quite three,
looking up to see,
you. Ma!
You were there,
on the terrace drying your hair.
I cannot remember what I felt,
just what I saw as I knelt,
on the flower bed below.
And so,
your last memory would be me.
Holding your swollen hand,
alone in alien ICU land,
singing you a childish song,
hoping you'd sing along.
I held it, till you went cold,
till they gently told
me – You were gone.
That was our circle, Ma.
Our own circle of life.
I began with you.
You ended with me.

Bhasha Dwivedi
Lucknow, India
Hour 2

Shunya

Dedicated to my father- Mr. Shishir Dwivedi

The Void
Nothingness
It exists
within me
and you, as well.
It makes up the space
we exist in
And the one
we can only dream of.
It connects
me to you
you to me.
Even with eons in between
my words reach
You
yours, Me
through Shunya
where everything exists
yet nothing remains.
Changes
in my heart
yours as well
the Only thing remaining
Unchanged
The Void
Nothingness.

(Shunya is a Hindi word, which means Zero. In the context of Indian Philosophical Thought, it also means the void, Space, vacuum and the Beginning among other things.)

Teresa Joswig
Stuttgart, Germany
Hour 11

Sourdough

Papa would bake
sourdough bread
twice a week,
and I'd always beg
for the hardened ends:
crispy, still steaming warm
melting anything spread
on top, and I'd always
eat it plain to savor
the cloud of taste left
by the crust.

Nowadays, Papa does
not bake anymore but he
still forms atmosphere
in the house by placing the needle
on every record he
decides to play on the
vintage phonograph that once
belonged to Oma.

Whenever the beat
gets too intense I'll see his eyes
turn periwinkle to forget-me-not,
face turn
sunflower to daisy,
hands turn
lily to geranium:
Papa becomes common
in grief, another broken man
walking to the grave of a person
who would not have let him cry.

Papa knows how to make good sourdough:
to keep a batch of it behind
to put into the next attempt at bread;
and to save spoonfuls of the next dough, also–
that is how he remembers Oma,
throws a spoonful of grief
into every day like it'll make it more digestible,
like he'll be able to bake
bread from it for a long time
if only he can make it last.

Kim Smart
Wall, South Dakota, USA
Hour 17

Hi from Heaven

You're here, I can smell you.
Nobody smokes at this house now,
but the smell of your cigarette hangs in the air,
as if you were still here

The pillows, I know I washed them.
Why do they smell like you?
Is this you aligned with that last instruction you gave
when you told me to always be brave?

And why is that ringtone blasting again?
It's not? I hear it.
And my phone is on silent.
Thank you for checking in.

You touched me again.
I felt it, on my shoulder and chin.
You do this, I know, to encourage me
when I feel so lonely again.

Christina Sng
Singapore
Hour 19

What's Left of Me

Hunger rumbles in my stomach
But my body does not want to move
From its resting state.

My mind still needs to replenish
From a decade of burning,
The ashes slowly dissipating.

I see so clearly now,
How I was destroyed,
What parts of me remain.

I pick up the remnants of myself,
Collect the shards of my heart,
And glue them back together,

Hoping they'll grow again.

Ofuma Agali
Lagos, Nigeria
Hour 1

Conferences and Confluence

i

Pains perch on parallel buds around us,
intersecting like painting gone wrong;
but they will flee, they will flee.
They may as well continue to nibble at us,
they will be doing so only to mock themselves;
for dawn will always come,
stretching from the opaque into the transparent,
mending the fences of reality.

ii

For Se:
The dark days never got through your doorsteps,
for your words wear a silk gown of bravery,
sweeping your floor clean,
as all sides of near-death receded
far and far away from your glow.
Silk and floor and life,
all sparkle;
breathing in whole-life,
deep and long,
in the sparkle.

iii

For Ingrid:
Those days of pain drowned
in the ocean of your love for nature.
Those images of the seas and the skies and the landscape,
they amplify the light your being feeds from.
Your external eyes are pretty, they already defeated the set back;
your inner eyes are bright, full of light,
full of life.

iv

For Caitlin:

86

Your inner strength is a moving mountain.
Light waves of agony do not prevail against mountains of life.
We will mock those pains and all its associated distractions.
Light waves of agony do not prevail against the laughters
that feed from your strength.

v
For Anjana:
That quarantine scare was a mere hoot
in the broken trunk of the scary trumpet.
The glow of your home is strong against the ills
of uncertainties flying like kites above us.
It is pretty clear we are not at its end.
It is pretty unclear we are in its middle.
Yet we live strong, ahead of the evening victories.
And your shout of relief sent a healing balm
across the conferences.

vi
For Mildred:
The chaos grew, swollen like the discarded dead.
Howl for the chaos;
I know, I know.
Howl...
If you are hanging in there, you are hanging well;
for dawn will always come.

vii
For Tanya:
How can pain not be scared
of the one who overcame it
over and over again?
You know your story, your story knows you.
Victory found you, got stuck with you.
Hold that grip, all the aces embrace you.
Victory will always find you,
even as gratitude dances for your living.

viii
For Jacob:
Great seeds sprout in silence.
They tower up high once above the surface.
With many fruits to spread around the globe,
yours is the manifestation of great harvests.
Many yet to come;
we will mock those pains, they cannot prevail.

ix:
For Tobe:
In a time of revisiting sorrows,
you savour the refreshing flow of the Vermont wind,
basking in the renewing words of converging poetry.
with chocolates drumming the echoes of time,
healing memories down the lane;
healing us all.

x
For Richard:
Seventieth is an upper landmark of life,
and there will be more decades of the line drawn with cheer.
In these conferences of poetry,
poems write us, you say.
As your words jet its healing all around us,
we await your twelve new surprises,
like a dozen denizens of poetic paradise.

xi
For us all:
Your voices are embraced with warmth when you speak.
Your silences are heard from across the horizons when you are mute.
All of us, as we chase essences in shapes and sizes,
we unite in these conferences, flowing into a confluence,
as we swim in the vast waters of unending renewal.

xii:
I sip from this cup of overflowing muses,
in these conferences,
converging into a confluence of communions.
All of the pains can nibble again.
They will be doing so only to mock themselves,
for dawn will always come.
Dawn will always come,
stretching from the opaque into the transparent,
mending the fences of reality.

Cinthia Albers
Maui, Hawaii, USA
Hour 16

Cat in the Window

Cat is spoiling my ocean-view.
He likes the open window
to watch the birds, the waves, the palms.
It is safe behind the window-screen
tucked behind the curtains
away from barking dogs
and the crows that squeal warnings
whenever he ventures outside.
He can watch the neighbors and not cower.
Here, he is the master.
His domain is small, fascinating.
He is vigilant.
Ready.
He blocks my ocean-view
but I get to watch him;
his head moving side to side
listening to invisible sounds,
sniffing the air for other peoples' dinners
feeling the ocean air caress his whiskers.
He is helping me write a poem.

Joshua Factor
Durham, North Carolina, USA
Hour 5

'til Kingdom Come

To all those who have come before,
I appreciate everything we've endured
lest we faded into an obscurity beyond comprehension. Don't
kill your darlings no matter how tempting
it may seem.
Never in existence or any type of
good place
did I imagine reencountering someone as
omni-benevolent as you, someone who
makes every day worth living, who
can make
our world a better and more
magnificent place just by existing. Thanks for just being you, for
everything.

Hope

Valarie Kirkwood
Topeka, Kansas, USA
Hour 17

Lonely Little Comfort Zone

Night falls against a stygian sky, until stars appear like pin holes of light.

The chartreuse shrouded moon makes me homesick for some low-
lit room.

The shrill call of locusts fills the night like a siren. I grasp the darkness
and shake it for fireflies.

Sleep is evasive and the deck beckons me. Peer upward it urges. Crickets
fall silent and traffic sounds fill the void, muddying the summer
ambience.

I try to reach up and grab a hunk of night, before clouds gathering in the
west spread, blinding the moon and shutting off the stars. As I skirt the
edge of midnight waiting for storms to arrive in the declining hours of
the morning, grumbling and flashing intermittent lightning, like furtive
glances. I can't manage a yawn.

I won't begrudge it the sweeping downpour that washes the world. I'll
find comfort in the darkness; I'll find joy in all the rain.

Jill Halasz
Texas City, Texas, USA
Hour 4

Tomorrow Is Another Day

"After all tomorrow is another day." - Margaret Mitchell, Gone with the Wind
(1936)
After all, tomorrow is another day.
This day's trials are passed.
While on this day, the struggle's real,
have faith it will not last.
For each new dawn is a new chance
to start over once more;
So, slumber deep with hope in sight
that only good's in store.

While yes, we only have the now
and tomorrow may spark fear,
the trials that you've survived this day -
each one has brought you here.
You've overcome this day! Congrats!
Be gentle with your mind.
You're stronger than you were before,
so leave the past behind.

Go forward in your slumber… deep.
Have dreams of what can be.
Keep peaceful thoughts in mind and sleep.
Knowing that you are free
of all this day's trouble abound –
Nothing's left in your way.
Reflect upon the courage you've found
for tomorrow is another day.

Margaret Saturley
Ybor City, Florida, USA
Hour 18

Whispers

When I am no longer here,
    just be still
    and listen.
You will hear my voice
    whispering in the wind.
What has been
    will always be.
Trust me.
Just be still
    and listen.

Julie Stanley
Upper Peninsula, Michigan, USA
Hour 1

Stay In The Moment

Wandering eyes with meandering mind
eat away at symbols
clutched within the web of thought.
I struggle and attempt to decipher,
yet every thought brings on more
questions than answers.
I bring myself back,
pulling myself down
out of the clouds,
and try and stay in the moment.
I see my reflection—
the tell-tale signs of age
and wisdom scurrying about the lines
drawn out by Father Time.
I smell the scent of freshly cut grass
billowing through the open window.
I taste the last drops of coffee
spilling down my chin—
caffeinated liquid gold.
I touch the hem of a shawl
wrapping around my fingers
in a lover's embrace—
protection from the cold, harsh world.
I listen to the silence.
The sound of alone.
The melody of my heartbeat…
I sink again into thought
as it yet still beats for you.
The daydreams clamber
up the mountains of sense
and finds that it makes none.

Does it matter?
I lose myself again in altitudes
only to force myself to ground
plummeting, like my heart
spiraling in a cacophony
of windswept imagination
and damnable overthinking.
Matching sequence to truth—
archeological digs brushing
away thought as I brush aside
yet another far-fetched dream,
trying to make sense of
ambiguity.
My restlessness is enjoying the ride
in disorienting travels from heaven
to earth,
and oft I wonder if I am
here or there?
In truth, I realize despite all that
I am both and everywhere.

Jessica Gershon
Covington, Tennessee, USA
Hour 3

Cross Over

Every garden deserves a bridge,
to symbolize the union,
walk across with courage,
connecting God and human.
Walking through the hardships,
feeling gaps of life and death,
when I cross over my heart skips,
and I can't catch my breath.
As I reach the other side,
hate becomes water under the bridge,
there is no divide,
only mistakes I will admit.
To surround myself in flowers,
are the seeds of change,
this garden is ours,
the bridge breaks the chains.

Kendra Reynolds
Northern Ireland
Hour 24

In Too Deep

Sometimes I dive too deep,
where water turns to liquid ice
and animals wear more serious skins
adapted to the harsh environment.

Sometimes I venture out
only to paddle in the shallows,
when that creature within
lures me out,
draws me down.

Losing control, I can only watch,
terrified and breathless,
while the water sets my body
rigid in muted panic.

Yet, always,
just as light begins to fade
and I feel my body drift untethered,
your hand reaches down
and gently plucks me out.

Hiral Bagadia
Vadodara, Gujarat, India
Hour 18

Self Rhyme

Just be still and listen,
self as a rhyme,
for you to be the morning reign,
and me your evening shine...
You to be the calmness of the moon,
I, the pace of the wind that is blown...
You be the dreams that come,
I, your bed lying comfortsome...
You be the thought to be done,
I, the support being the power before it's gone...
You to be the direction of life,
I, your signage on each of the sight...
You to be the purpose to survive,
I, the reason for it to strive...
You to be the silver line in the absence of light,
I, to support its shine, enhancing its bright...
You to be the support in each of life's talks,
I, your shadow accompanying all of your walks...
You to be the center of universe,
I, the planet revolving forward and reverse...
You so are the life's sunshine,
I, to carry all the ruskiness as you define...

Ashley "LuvMiFreely" Powers
Dayton, Ohio, USA
Hour 9

This Too Shall Pass

The world has been sitting on my shoulders
I feel my posture dragging
I'm often told I must pick myself up
They don't know how often I pick up the pieces
But every shattered piece cuts me
So, I'd rather leave them on the ground
Every time a wound heals
Something replaces the pain
Until I become numb
I'm told that I'm strong
They fail to notice that I'm weak in my stance
But God holds me up when I'm at my weakest
The world knocks me down
I throw in the towel
He throws it back
Tells me to wipe my tears
Stands me back on my feet
Then He gloves up and takes on my battles
So, although my flesh wants to give in
My spirit reminds me that I'm built in His image
This too shall pass

Simona Frosin
Bucharest, Romania
Hour 10

Miraculous

I found a time capsule, can you believe it?
And inside it was a tiny fairy, she told me
that she survived due to the power of hope.
Somehow I understood everything she said.

I was mesmerized, she was happy to share.
She said that she was born out of a lullaby
and that a powerful princess sent her here
to guard the dreams of those encountered.

It was the princess's gift to a planet losing faith.
I was really happy to meet her and I felt blessed.
She left to be the guardian of others' dreams too,
not before adding that I can keep her in my heart!

Hearts

Cynthia Hernandez
Bremerton, Washington, USA
Hour 1

A Reluctant Goodbye

A reluctant goodbye
    hung suspended
        in the space between us:

a held breath
    an undelivered kiss
        a question with no answer

the trembling recognition of grace
    and hands that want to hold on
        —even as they're letting go.

Tobe Zalinger
Vermont, USA
Hour 5

Reflection

All my lovers were worth it,
even when I cried and tried
to understand why they left
or stopped being kind.

I had them, each at their best
and most wonderful, when they
were full of pride and beauty.
 I was their proven prize.

In time I would become wise
to their protected self.
While slowly, being revealed,
their bitterness grew.

Finally discarded like
an old mirror, reflecting
an imperfect vision,
relieved, they let me go.

Through the looking glass
I am able to see fragments
of that girl they had won.
Remembering, she smiles back.

JR Turek
Chicago, Illinois, USA
Hour 24

Dove Chocolates

I sense a theme here, check the bag,
good until December, still 6 months
away, no festive pictures on the bag;
not stale, they are as decadent as
I remember.

Without warning, another
Bring in the holiday together
and here I have to gather willpower,
seal the bag and wonder
what holiday
together
with whom?

Not as inspirational as I'd hoped, but
an intoxicating, delectable, wanton way
to de-stress. Ok, maybe just one more
if I can unwrap the layers of packing tape
I wound around it, unstick the super glue,
and remove staples without stabbing myself.

On second thought, the bag is already sealed
and it will stay fresh until December.

Yeah, let's see how long that will last.

Katie Dunne
Chicago, Illinois, USA
Hour 24

I wish I had the stars

that lit our midnight walk,
boot prints in snow, broken
bridges holding our dance.

I wish I had the stars

that I saw in your eyes,
twinkle of the Dipper
reflected on your car.

I wish I had the stars

to guide me back to God,
show He never fails, loves –
stars of your goodnight kiss.

Renee A. Perkins
Washington DC, USA
Hour 16

What Must I Do?

Tell me what you want me to do
Tell me the answer that will release me
I tire of your games, your unending riddles

What must I say, what must I do, to be free of you?

You contend I have entombed you
I contend you have entombed yourself
You yearn for freedom? Then free yourself.

What must I say, what must I do, to be rid of you?

You dare pretend victim
Allege prey to my predator
Enough of your lies

What must I say, what must I do, to be free of you?

I pretend nothing
I am prey to no one
Lies tumble from your tongue alone.

What must I say, what must I do, to be rid of you?

I beg you, please, grant my liberation
You've stolen my life
I would think that would suffice you

What must I say, what must I do, to be free of you?

How does one steal an offered life?
Gaze in the mirror and behold your executioner.
Forgive yourself and free us both.

Ermelinda Makkimane
Goa, India
Hour 17

rain revelation

the downpour begins
as suddenly as it had stopped
we rush for shelter
we've been silly -
leaving home without rain wear
in a hurry to buy groceries
now we stand
under the awning
of a small shop
watching the raging
stream of rainwater
rushing past our feet
you stand calm
and i wonder if you
remember that day
a similar awning
two silly new adults
couldn't keep their hands
off the other
the shopkeeper had
to shoo them away
like he would do to stray dogs
coupling in the middle of the street
they ran off
one giggling
the other smiling broadly
into the pouring rain
inviting stares
from the sheltering people
and the odd dog

i give you the same
sidelong glances
as i had on that day
i want to ask you
if you remember
what you remember
but you don't notice my cues
you're quiet
as if gauging some
inner storm
the rain lowers gears
becomes a drizzle
we sit on the scooter
drenched
and drive off
barely touching

Thryaksha A Garla
Chennai, India
Hour 1

The Circle's Endings and Beginnings (A Reverse Poem)

Endings.
Peace and quiet.
They're anything but,
The raging storm that breaks through a ship.
They're the grand culmination that completes your journey
I would be lying if I ever dared to say to you that,
I hate them with my whole heart.
I adore them so.
I look in the mirror as I lie that,
Endings are just chaos and fire reigning the town,
Bringing the circle to a close.
But a circle does not end,
But a circle does not begin,
Sketching the first dot of the circle.
Mishaps and everyone finding their footing.
I'd be lying if I say that beginnings are only,
Small gasps of surprise and happiness.
They're taxing and eating through your soul.
They aren't just the first thing that comes to mind that,
They're the adrenaline keeping you young.
Leaving your comfort space you call home.
They're anything but,
Peace and quiet.
Beginnings.

Megan Saturley
Orlando, Florida, USA
Hour 9

One Glance

Sun-kissed skin,
strawberry eyes,
white chocolate smile,
nectarine skies.
Mango lips,
cocoa breeze,
just one glance at her
brings me to my knees.

Nandiya Nyx
Philadelphia, Pennsylvania, USA
Hour 17

Last Night

Last night together
walking over Whangarei
bridge. Finally, the truth.

Ramona Jones
St. Petersburg, Florida, USA
Hour 12

Invisibly Lonely

Solitary

Unfrequented

Remote

I had to be born this way

Or else it wouldn't feel so natural

It gives me time to reflect,

Makes me who I am…

I am not invisible.

Session

I saw through your soul at first sight,
soulless soul,
hollow as mine.
Tiger's spirit; Judge, jury and executioner,
rolled into one ball of calm fury.

Seeking me out for my own travesties,
Such is the nature of your calling.
Next on your list,
my penchant for the death dramatis a failing,
at least to you.

Appointment made, counselling the lies,
in each word of deceit sits a truth,
I am as naked to you as you are to me.
Both eluding the authorities,
failing to offer expected motive.

Motive is desire, nothing more,
seekers of sanctions and retribution,
unleashing a fury on the troubling.
We are natural born killers,
punishing the unworthy.

You try to deny the thrill, justify with just cause,
whereas I consume my prey in part,
dress the rest as a side dish for all to see.
I hear your hollow words,
but I listen to the unspoken.

The recorder is switched off, the papers stowed,
I lean forward locking my eyes with yours,
'your words are gracious mendacities. I see you.
Renowned for my discretion, speak freely,
as a sheep who addresses the silent priest.

For there is much we have in common,
baying for the blood of the unrighteous,
bringing justice where justice fails.
open yourself to me, offer the truth,
and we shall seek together.'

Brett Dyer
Galway, Ireland
Hour 2

Illusion of Similarity

I feel eloquent corruption stirring within.
A vacant void filled with ravenous curiosity,
for I see the inhuman suit before, from me;
A pure manifestation of my purest desire.
The vacancy within myself screaming,
writhing in its silent symphony of macabre lust,
coiled in on itself with immoral delight,
patient in its own blood rapture to come.

The facsimile of humanity that sits adjacent to me,
scrutinizing myself as her own unadulterated image,
stilled acknowledgement of her duplication of death.

My heart calm and steady in your glare.
most people go through life devoid of what we share;
A common ground of vicious aspirations,
the purest form of balanced damnation our calling,
the dissimilar methods of no consequence.

I address the would-be beast of prey before me,
monotones of jovial unconcern ringing out,
A gambit of normality to snare my inhuman prey.

The game commences with appropriate discord,
'A common cause does invite strange bedfellows,
seeking what we both desire from anti-life.
The greatest form of scales to be balanced,
and always at the end of my equity bringing hand.
Perhaps we shall both enjoy the other's company of carnage,
soulless in its own rapture of screams.'

Seeking the demise of the unjust,
my own form circling yours,
drawing the chaos akin to the fly,
as the normality of a spider will ensnare you.

In time

Laurie McKay
Northern Lower Peninsula, Michigan, USA
Hour 4

How to Say Goodbye*

As family gathers,
we say goodbye
for hours, or so it seems.
It's been so long
since we've said hello
and we're welcomed into this world.

Now we stand,
with aching arms,
holding heavy, sleepy big girls.
Arms aching with weight;
arms aching with emptiness,
as we say goodbye.

Caught swaying
– teetering in limbo.
Between staying and going,
car and house,
struggling.
Longing for a clue of how to say goodbye.

Of how to say everything needed to be said,
while loosening our grip on everything that will never be
heard,
spoken,
discussed,
again.

Hugs ending too soon,
constricted throats
and watery eyes,
and attempts at smiled reassurance.
Hoping to calm
the curious wide-eyed worry of the young,
without having to voice lies about
'being fine' or 'it will be okay.'

How we say goodbye
through laughter and witness.
Hand-holds released
to wipe away snot and tear streaked faces.
Sobbing with the inability to detach
or accept
the surreal-ness
Of how to say goodbye.

*"How to say goodbye."
Tyler, Anne. Ladder of Years. New York. Ballantine Books. 1995. p. 326

Amber L. Crabtree
Mesa, Arizona, USA
Hour 17

Like They Do in The Books

I wanted to spend the rest of my life
loving him in ways no other human
could possibly love him.
Much like people do in sultry novels.

For that, I learned the strength he hides
in the push and pull of his tides,
and how fickle the waves of his emotions
could be.

When he assured me that he is not
"needy like other Cancers",
I should have known that he would be
as icy and aloof as my own Cancerian heart.

These revelations have not deterred me
from loving him, but they have reminded
me that loving people is not the same as
loving books.

Habitat

Katie Scholan
Bristol, United Kingdom
Hour 21

Winter

The crows were paper cut-outs against the light,
The tree an ink spill.
Their voices cut-out voices as they took their flight
Whilst the birds in the hedgerow trailed watercolours.

The endless clouds were writer's block,
Dampness eating through the page,
And at the skyline, bleeding up,
The church towers leaked villages.

In shattered fields, between the trees,
Beneath the troubled sky,
Barley was vivid only as a memory.
And the frost built sparkling sculptures too ephemeral.

Sandy Lender
Central Florida, USA
Hour 18

Honeybees

crafting questions
to question my talent
vibrant colors
cover inadequacies
in technique
and mixing of media

above the canvas
buzzing bees
bring me a smile
reminding me
of dragonflies
checking a child's coloring chart
way back when I was seven

maybe my art
bold in its yellow
amber
and gold
isn't a complete loss
if I can fool the honeybees
into checking it out

Deanna Ngai
Airdrie, Alberta
Hour 12

Summertime Blaze

Drenched in the heat of the daytime sun
I find myself feeling drowsy.
I stretch and yawn in my chair
with skin that's red and warm.
The heat lingers on
even as I
slink inside
to cool
me.

Rajani Nair
Kuala Lumpur, Malaysia
Hour 3

Sole

I see the world through the lens,
it is a different shade every time;
no matter how much I visualise,
it is always at its prime.

As I tread along the path,
and soak in the beauty around;
I wish I could stay on here,
immense peace I have found.

I know not what I will do,
when I have to move away;
it will always be in my heart,
I'll never forget it, I pray.

As I stand here amidst,
this vivid scenic bliss;
I want time to stand still,
there's nothing else I would miss.

I see everyone around,
has a lens for them to see;
they have a world they built,
just like I have, for me!

As you watch me from there,
I know you see me sole;
in my world I am the queen!
No one else plays that role.

Cindy Thompson
Lakewood, Colorado, USA
Hour 23

Catching Fireflies

That magical moment each summer
when the first fireflies appeared,
blinking me, winking me out of the house.
Jar in hand,
stealthily advancing,
trapping one and then another.
Illuminated glass glows,
a mystic lantern,
a tragic prison.
By morning's light,
their bioluminescence extinguished,
tiny bodies lie in repose.
Now, years later,
I blame my unfortunate luck in love
on my errant firefly actions.
Surely I am being punished
for lacking an all-creatures-great-and-small
respect for Mother Nature.
Atonement will come only
if I instruct my own children
in the art of catch and release.
But I simply can't rob them
of the childhood ritual
of lightning bug delight
in a jar.

Roxann Harvey-Lawrence
Jamaica
Hour 24

Disaster in the Tropics

Life has paused
Nothing seems to be moving
Life is on stand still
Change is coming
Where is the bill?

Great thoughts arise
Panting and searching
For the prize
Where is this strange demise
Seems it's bigger in size?

Questions unanswered
Life is on pause
Let's hustle up
For the cause

Shirley Durr
Minneapolis, Minnesota, USA
Hour 20

Walking the Night

"I have been one acquainted with the night.
... I have outwalked the furthest city light"
(From "Acquainted with the Night" by Robert Frost)

No remote nature road for me
Where small rustles in the grass chill my gut,
Where moon and stars play hide and seek
Behind brooding verdant branches;
Where cackling cicadas watch over me,
Warning me they are waiting.

Spare me the desolation
Where something howls at the sky;
Where my lonely steps
Crush the paths I walk.
Where friends are empty echoes
Of memory.

Give me city lights in my night,
Solitude in a crowd,
Feeding all my senses:
Reverberating voices tripping over each other,
Smoky roastings tempting my tongue,
Blasts of heat and rot beneath,
Colors rioting beyond the rainbow.

Give me the city
Where wishing stars
And moonlight larger than the sun,
Play along the asphalt;
Where other walkers and I make music
Like jazz, dancing our variations,
Watching each other prance
In the glowing darkness;
Where I hear laughs of mirth,
Sobs of grief, hums of life.

Ami Gypsie Offenbacher-Ferris
Wilmington, North Carolina, USA
Hour 6

Wheels

I cannot run
I cannot hide
I cannot go down a children's slide

You can do this, and I can do that
What I can do, others can not
I can race across a hot parking lot

Both of your feet would blister and burn
Those with two legs, two feet and a spine
Could never keep up with these two wheels of mine

As you lumber to find your way
One foot down and the other just so
I'm wheeling round and round, to and fro

To soar like a king or dance like a queen
Moving across that marbled dance floor
I can keep going and want more and more

When 'ere your limbs become leaden and sore
Mine do not tire, I do not fret
My legs do not cramp when riding a jet

It's blessed that I am and blessed that I'll be
'Tis only at night when the whippoorwill calls
that I honestly don't think about it much at all

In that darkest of dark within nights deepest night
When my soul soars forth and struggles to fly
It's only then I look down and wonder why

What did I do to earn such a fate
To all I am kind, loving and fair
Then why am I tied to this blasted wheelchair

131

Amy Laird
Spencer, Iowa, USA
Hour 21

Night Owl

It's so quiet now
no traffic
no harsh lights
no demands on my time
no people

Perfect time to write
plenty of stillness
for inspiration
I have what I need for a night
such as this

Cold shiver as I
start to prepare to
dive into this hole
the journey of which
is hard to explain

If you've never done it
you won't understand
the exhilaration
the painful
tough
annoying
raw
bleeding
process that it can be

I can't explain it to you

Quietly, patiently
trying to sketch out
the thoughts in my head

some come easy, others take time

132

others will not come at all
like loosening a tight bolt

There!
what's that
A spark of thought
image to start
a distant sound
mournful cry

plain paper
easiest to gather
thoughts on
walking restlessly

couldn't sleep tonight
guess that's why I'm
tucked here on the floor
against this old wall
not really tired though

I can almost hear the clock
in the hall ticking away the time

Running out of time
almost out of time
I can imagine it screaming

But that's OK

I am in control
I set the pace
and that's OK

Another bite of inspiration
this one delicious
yet dark and taunting

dipping into the dangerous
flirting with scary
what was that cold shiver for?

This spark scares me-
it's going to take me
someplace I don't want to go
but that's beauty of my craft-
everything's ripe for use

I can see it getting lighter out
now, the night is almost over-
I don't know what to do-
I have so much more left
that needs to be said

Calm yourself
you'll be OK
the night will come again
and there you'll be

I can hear noise now
people getting up
ready to start their day

meanwhile I'm here
putting my craft to bed-
setting a reminder of
where I stopped-

Just to pick it up once more.

Jarrod Fouts
Griffin, Georgia, USA
Hour 14

Skyscrapers

They said we never would, so we finally did
by that time, we were all already dead
just waiting for the light to show up and take us
it didn't, so the brewing rage boiled over

I showed you how to make a good fire
the gas canister pulled you down with it
until you emptied it in the lobby
there were so many around us, laughing
and when the sparks lit up a smile, I knew I loved you

The suited men, for all their millions, couldn't fly
they rained from the tops of the skyscrapers like well-dressed rubble
I held your ears in my hands because it bothered you, the way they hit
and with my mouth I kissed your dirty forehead

The skyline was beautiful on fire
the shadows danced on the smoke clouds above
as if the great beast was dying before us, finally after all this time
I held your hand and we cheered a new world, one rising from the rubble
where we would be something.

Dexta Jean Rodriquez
Russellville, Arkansas, USA
Hour 20

particularly in the summer, I love to noctambulate
seems that all of creation, both God's and man's, are pulling us outdoors
blame it on the stars, the moon, the city lights
or blame no one but ourselves
for being attracted to the shiny parts
interspersed among the long shadows

Gina Gil
Arlington, Virginia, USA
Hour 21

Ode to the South River

Wrapped in colors of sunrise, cloaked in morning mist, elegant mistress with
your siren call = irresistible, and engaged without regrets.
Never do I wish I hadn't stepped on your shores. Slipped into your embrace.

Whether cold, dark, warm, or bright = no matter. Sure, I lingered at
water's edge a little longer at daybreak in October. When I finally put my
face in the water, my breath whisked away, forehead wrinkled with the
pain of sinuses and brain frozen, temporarily.

This is only testimony to my adoration.
There are plenty of days without frigid temperatures to be had.
It's just that if entry is possible, I will not resist.

Every visit brings revelations and glorious experiences with nature, with
friends, with self. I glide through the surface waters = some days are still
as glass
and some bring the motion of hills crossing over you.
The salt waxes and wanes.

The group close enough to be together but with space to thrive. The
bright colored buoys bob across the water
and mark each friend, each one dedicated
to sport or love of water.

Conditions ever-changing. Life greets us with osprey diving for meals,
gulls circling and gliding nearby,
and the one touchy, feely type that connects with burning irritation.
Not welcome, but tolerated, as the cost we pay to be in her presence.

Even with the jellies' sting, I always am glad to swim in the South River.
The container, the medium, the place
for my communion with the water and the swimmers.

Angie Mountain
Ambler, Pennsylvania, USA
Hour 16

Fire Song

I love to watch the flames
In a blazing campfire
Tangle together, then
Leap apart
In a dance that never repeats,
Yet remains the same,
Never failing to entrance.
There's depth to a campfire.
More than just how it looks.
More that fascinates and captivates,
That mesmerizes and tantalizes.

Warmth, of course.
Heat.
Drawing me in,
Pushing me away.
The wanting to be close,
The needing to find space.

The smell of wood burning,
Of hickory, in particular,
Bringing me back home,
Sitting nearby as my father feeds
Wedges of wood, too fast,
Onto a fire
In a home-fashioned rusted iron pit.

Lacking oxygen, the fire
Sends out a call for help — smoke,
Rolling off the wood and
Catching flight,
Reaching for the chance to escape.
The campfire supplying musical
Accompaniment for its dance.

The sharp scrape of the match
Signaling the opening stanza.
Eerie silence, a collective

Held breath, hoping for success.
Air blown softly,
Then greater puffs,
Then the faint, unmistakable whoosh
Of flame climbing,
Spreading, pulling twigs into the song.

Sizzling harmonies underlie the notes
As water in the wet wood gives up
And waltzes into the fray.
The occasional "Crack!" dividing
the measures into stanzas, verses,
As the melody spins its way
onto the cool evening air.

And finally, as the whirling music fades
Into a dusky lullaby,
One last, long, loud hiss,
The water thrown, reluctantly,
Over the faint red of the slumbering coals,
Plunging all into silence,
Into darkness,
Into the cold
Of night.

William Jackson (willjxn)
Saratoga Springs, Utah, USA
Hour 23

Droplets of Seraphic Light

Droplets of seraphic light
the camera froze up time for you.
Glowing abdomens so bright,
dance around the tall bamboo.

I would like to join in play,
dapple light along my way.

Little seraphs tipped with light,
see me through this pitch-dark night.

Lee Montgomery
Stevenson, Scotland
Hour 4

The Other Wind

(after Ursula Le Guin)

not yet ... he said
the time is not right
the earth is unaligned
the sacred path unknown
dreams come
from beyond the wall of separation
incursions of the dead
stalk the living
seeking freedom
shapeshifters
dragons
walking among the living
their destination ... Earthsea

Half Marathon Poems

Moments

Anwar Suleman
Johannesburg, South Africa
Hour 11

GOD'S CANVAS

On the canvas of the sky
is splashed with different shades of darkness,
giving way to hues of pink, red and burnt orange
as the sun begins to peep from
behind the backdrops of the majestic mountains.

The rays of the sun steal from the darkness,
the canvas of the earth is tinged
with subtle shades of browns and greens,
the living painting of the trees and plants
become apparent and focused.

The paint brush of the sun,
traverses with gentle but deliberate strokes upon the sky,
the deep, dangerous sea begins to
shimmer and sparkle, invitingly.

No doubt, natures crescendo of colours
And subtle shades have been painted by
The Master Painter, God Almighty!

Lovers' Contentment

Under the periwinkle sky
We decipher shapes in the clouds,
Ignoring the pine needles under our backs
And finding the beat in the cicada hum
Let's spread this moment across forever

Maria Riofrio
New York, New York, USA
Hour 8

Mute

Silence is not golden;
at this moment
as all words fail me
it is a pounding, penetrating reminder
of failure.

The air conditioner comes on from time to time
my sole sound companion
as it achieves its blustering drone
I just want it to stop.
I can take the heat but not the monotony
too much of my present predicament.

I find no comfort in being alone with my thoughts
when the thoughts do not come
when the ideas that flowed and crested
swirl to a standstill
then crash
against an invisible dam-

A beaver's wet dream.

Outside my window
the wind advances across the wide street below
battle-ready for the coming storm
it takes no prisoners and gives not one damn
if only I had that courage
to set these letters free.

Brenda DeHaan
Wagner, South Dakota, USA
Hour 7

normal or not

normal now is not
normal pre-2020
new vision for all

Naida Supnet
Pasig City, Philippines
Hour 1

Chasing Norma

On the third month of twenty-twenty one
we chased time ...we did chase time
We chased time, all of us, to keep you with us
but chasing time was not enough.

Your time on earth, your time is up
We lost you, our base, our rock,
Losing your every embrace
Something that won't be replaced

You are our core we are left shattered
and every day we're lost and bothered
Chase your dreams you keep telling us
Do good things and don't make a fuss

We might have lost in chasing time
We might have lost you physically
But your memories will come in rhyme
Your love and all will be in prime

Chasing you mother, Norma your sweet name
You might have left... who else to blame
Your words and wisdom will all remain
Us, your children will see you again.

We chased time to chase your life but we lost
We only have your love, your words and anecdotes
Chasing you, Mother, there's nothing we can do.
We'll just confine you in our hearts, by then, we'll get through.

Adriana Grant
Somerville, Massachusetts, USA
Hour 6

Walking

feet feet, legs stride, a gait
gazing, sky is always ever
above, cloud companions,
a parallel movement, step-step,
foot-fall, foot-fall, arms swing,
swinging, the moving of the body
slow, regular, the way a body
picks itself up, one foot, one
half, one side at a time,
and then gives that half back
to the ground, sidewalk, street,
forest, beach. A body takes
itself apart, balancing one
half, other half, a spine
jointing the halves to ease.
forward there are weeds.

151

JC Reilly
Marietta, Georgia, USA
Hour 11

Twilight

Let it come, the periwinkle spread of first twilight,
when the fireflies are just starting their light show,
and the membrane of clouds begins to thin
like the windowpane test for good sourdough,
enough to let the timid stars catch you off-guard,
like the flutter of eyelashes from a pretty girl.

Cue the cicadas, cue the crickets who will chirp
just to keep you company. While the dark birds
hang on the electrical wires, like musical notes,
you will rock in your hammock and be content—
nothing can needle you now, not even mosquitoes.
You could not ask for more—you're not that greedy.
When a breeze sneaks in like a child after curfew,
this is what you live for each summer, this moment.

Davion Moore
Sandusky, Ohio, USA
Hour 11

My First Nonet

Today, I embarked on something new,
and stepped out of my comfort zone
To try something different
is a courageous act,
not everyone does.
Is it scary?
Yes, it is.
But it's
Done.

Brian Hasson
Derry City, Northern Ireland
Hour 12

Young Lady

I knew from the first moment, my heart
instantly fell in complete love
with the soul of a truly
genuine young lady.
There I'll always be
if ever you
need me. You
have my
word.

Sheila Sondik
Bellingham, Washington, USA
Hour 10

A Litany

If we were lucky enough
lucky enough in the pandemic
in the pandemic we survived
we survived quite comfortably
quite comfortably we were full of angst
we were full of angst and counted
and counted our blessings
our blessings were many and great
many and great we acknowledge
we acknowledge and yet we fear
we fear for the future
over which we have no control
no control and let us say
(fill in the blank)

Kathleen (Kat) Kidder
Nashville, Tennessee, USA
Hour 11

Ranger's Autumn Duty

Autumn.
A mixed bag for a forest ranger.
Clouds floating over
a periwinkle sky,
no clue they offer
of the danger nearby.
Nature's golden-green pallet spread
across a pine-needle floor makes a bed
under trees wrapped in vines of ivy,
touching the sky.
Sensing the air, dusty and dry,
gumboots heavy,
lifeless leaves beat
into the clay beneath his feet.
Ignoring the smoldering stench.
His focus today is to quench
flickering flames, before
they reach a weathered door.

Miggy Faeder
England
Hour 4

Burning Salt

"And the ashes blew towards us with the salt wind from the sea"
after Daphne Du Maurier

And the ashes blew towards us with the salt wind from the sea
And the burning fell about, the debris landing at our feet
I have never felt so open to the elements, so seen
By emptiness in cracks as they split between their seams
The boat is dressed in red now, the body must be gone
The flames have eaten everything, it didn't take them long
Let's hope she isn't carried in the waves way out to sea
What's left will billow upwards, what's left will always be
Let's hope that she disintegrates and falls into the sky
At least this way, we get a final chance to say goodbye

Sundar Walker
Lancashire, England
Hour 11

The Yew Tree

Go and plant a tree,
it is our wedding anniversary
I certainly will I said
I went and bought a Golden Yew
it's foliage for me
and berries for you!
The Yew is fifty years old
is always covered in green and gold,
it's berries twinkle in the Sun
much loved and admired by everyone!

A mistle thrush comes
to the Yew Tree
and sings its song for you and me
each evening so
sweetly and so long
renews our ties each
year anew
for you and me
and the golden Yew.

Vidya Shankar
Chennai, India
Hour 12

Pillow Talk (a zuihitsu)

birds on my mango tree beat their wings, sing early morning chants
curtains in my bedroom flutter with the early morning breeze
my eyes blink rapidly from being awake all night

the world pulls me to its chores
my pillow beckons
maybe some coffee?

chole for lunch
ginger, garlic, *jeera*, cinnamon,
pepper, cloves, *kasuri methi*, red chilli, turmeric
      blend
      store
      add generously

will my yearning for the pillow unspice the *chole*?

the whirr of the fan
loud enough to disrupt conversation in my head
sings me a lullaby

the glorious sun, at radiant best

help me embrace sleep

*chole: a spicy Indian dish

Nancy Canyon
Bellingham, Washington, USA
Hour 7

The Change

When you say *normal*   you think about   the past
& the things you depended upon   & the things that stayed the same
then you   learned that change   was the only thing   that you
could depend upon   you learned that you could resist   or you
could let go   & be thankful   when   isolation arrived again
you had to adjust   to change   alone in your room   you worked
the *new norm*   people said when you met   on ZOOM
some said the weather was never this hot   or smoky   & they said
they were scared   & once again   you recalled what
it used to be like   & thought   this is a new life   move on
be the change   make art   read   write   make love   adapt.

Manoshi Bose
India
Hour 9

The Secret

Once in a blue moon,
I take out an old picture of myself
just to check how many wrinkles I've added
since I crossed happy days

Once in a blue moon,
I try to recollect just what you whispered
into my ears as we made love
but all that echos is the crack of a sharp slap across my face

Once in a blue moon,
I drink wine from the flute
just to remind myself that its cracked, sharp edge
can no longer press against my throat as I'm backed far up against the
wall

Once in a blue moon,
I use my silver brush to smoothen my silver strands
They lost their dark colour too soon, but my dark secret...
that will last my lifetime and a little more

Once in a blue moon,
I walk downstairs into the cellar
to check for the stench of yesterday
but the rats seem to have wiped away every inch of you!

Daryl Curnow
Auckland, New Zealand
Hour 9

Soak

Soft water gels over your body
soothing your skin
washing troubles away
you look out to the city and ponder...
What is everyone else doing? I soak here

relaxed

what troubles are they going through?
do I care? Am I supposed to care?
I think not
it soothes my skin, this water
just what I needed

I can see my reflection
almost better than a mirror
it's wavy
just like life
there are no straight lines.

Buried Truth

Aching to see you;
I wonder what could be,
the catalyst for your heart,
to gently reach for me.

Aching to see you;
I know it's been too long,
since your mind found peace,
since your soul has reached the dawn.

An *aching to see* truth,
is where the rest will start;
For the *ache* is only Glory

— An invitation *to see[k]* the truth in *you[r]* own heart.

Harvey Schwartz
Bellingham, Washington, USA
Hour 3

Unfiltered

How much of me is unfiltered?
How much of me is intrinsic?

Or, am I a compilation of people I've
known and admired or had issues with?

Smart kids in college.
Athletes in high school.
Winners with the girls.
That completely relaxed
go-with-the-flow guy.

Someone whose ideas I love
but would never have thought
of in a million zillion years.

How much of me is unfiltered?

The Marlboro man puffing with certainty.
Babe Ruth pointing to the stands.
The crazy politician who seems so certain.

How much of me is unfiltered?

Each day could drip newness
as if our abundant Northwest rain
washes away the old me over and over and over.

Much of me is unfiltered.

because all my huge decisions,
the ones that changed my life
the ones I talk about reverentially
that may bore those around me who
have heard the story one too many times…

were shots of lightning
blasted from the canon
of imagination freed from
the fear of doing something wrong.

Heidi G. Browning
Salt Lake City Region, Utah, USA
Hour 6

Vast

Deep oceans quench sandy shores as
tides roll in,
out,
masking waters troubled by
fish in swaying anemones, hiding from
lurking enemies – demons
of the deep.
Life diving, fleeing, fighting,
searching –
unknown cerulean depths beneath

untroubled celestial skies,
refuge for traveling clouds brushed
by unseen breeze and soaring
silhouettes.
Soon sapphires will leisurely roll,
revealing unhurried rubies and
flecks
of gold,
then coal-backed diamond
stars.

Your eyes hold a universe of possibilities.

Robbie West
Bernkastel-Kues, Germany
Hour 12

My Own Path

All my life I have gone my own way.
It's a lonely path filled with traps
and dangers but also joy.
Because ever present
in times of sorrow,
in times of strength,
self-respect
dwells in
me.

James Featherstone
Herrin, Illinois, USA
Hour 6

Pandora's Box

Monster inside.
Fighting to be free.
A black dragon,
shiny and sleek.

Don't let him out.
Into the world he flies,
with wings spread.
A shadow blotting out the sun.

It feels good to be out.
Go anywhere, do anything.
Be who I want to be.
Have all the things.

Watch out, the beast is loose.
Pandora's box is broken.
I will never be caged,
ever again.

Susan Hannon
Palm Springs, California, USA
Hour 10

Moment in Time

The lights twinkle
at the neighborhood diner in Chicago
announcing it's
Christmas time.
She sits across from me
with her manic self,
talking and laughing non-stop
while I watch her,
exhausted by her energy.
She's excited and I'm glad
but it's a little too much,
a bit too forced.
And I know all this energy
will spiral downwards
in the new year.
But right now,
it's Christmas time.

Leroy Leonard
Centennial, Colorado, USA
Hour 11

A POETRY MARATHON LIMERICK

A manic young poet named Moore,
Penned poems 'til his butt became sore.
He was prompted, at last,
To rescue his ass,
Because Grubhub had come to the door.

Bavishya S
Chennai, India
Hour 12

Dawn at Chennai

I hear caws and coos and chirps and clicks
I feel the cold breeze on my skin
There is a red dot rising
Behind the silhouette
Of silent buildings
In the city
People call
Modern
Home

David Hirsh
Nassau County, New York, USA
Hour 4

However you conclude
We will applaud
Some will stand
Others will stay sitting
The sound of your voice
Carries across the hall
Built for acoustic marvels
I, myself, am in awe
This is the third time
I've seen you recite
And each time
My mind dwells
In the words
I know so well
I wander around
With you
On your journey
Through the cities
And the places where people dwell
And the forests
Where trees, animals and forces of nature dwell
You show photographs
For those who need
Visual assistance
I prefer the words
That dwell between the silence
That live because you know how to hesitate
You talk about how you were almost hit by lightning
As a metaphor
And how you took long walks
To avoid playing cards all night
You were an avid loser at poker
Although you could read the other players

You felt bad for them
You weren't that kind of killer
You would take a camera with you
And write about the pictures you took
And show those pictures as a slide
But I would rather hear the silence
Between the words
Than see what happened
To the tree you hid under
To avoid the rain
After it was hit by lightning
And continued to smoke in the fog.

Pea Flower Tomioka
Singer Island, Florida, USA
Hour 2

After a Playlist on my Morning Run

There is salt in the air here.

I can taste it, breathing, alive in my mouth.
It feeds against the rhythm underneath me.
There is a golden dawn ahead, and the edges of this
silence breaking across diamonds is yet unpunished.
I feel the earth shift under my toes.

His voice is magic I carry in labeled jars.
They fill my ears with beeswax when I unscrew the lids
and hold them up to forgotten doorways.
He slips secrets inside the honeycomb.
I will suckle at them from chipped ceramics
when I make my evening tea.

My heart is a drumbeat against the shoreline.
I can feel the rising pulse of heat behind his breaking kiss.
It punches through and the sea is afire with his need.
I wonder if she burns under these kisses.
I wonder if this is how muses are born.

I am incomplete without these rituals.
I only know the secrets I wash from my feet.
The musings and gifts are not mine to open.
But I will stand witness to his voice, in traditions
like meditation, to repeat a trick where
one day, I too will reach some peace.

Gita Bharath
Chennai, India
Hour 10

Wake up, Gita!

I know it's Sunday, but the hours will not keep.
Do not waste this day in unfeeling sleep.
There's so much to do, much to see—
birds building nests, although the trees
stand undressed in the yard.

On weekdays you have jobs to do,
but today, you can frolic in the dew,
drink from a raindrop caught in a leaf,
wonder at the cicada's unerring belief
that seventeen years are gone. Why
would you want the world to pass you by
when you can shout and laugh and cry
out loud to the clear blue sky?

Aishwarya Vedula
Chhattisgarh, India
Hour 12

Blurred Destiny

One fine morning, crisp mist gathered my
senses, mainly my vision got
blurred, forming a fragile lens.
Lens of prism, scattering
hallucinations
of destiny
desired
once.

Sandra de Helen
San Diego County, California
Hour 10

Winter Solstice

A favorite winter holiday,
Earth reaches the farthest point
from the sun.

The longest night signals
the long sleep underground
for plants that will rise again

in the spring. It is the time
we put away the outdoor tools,
take up knitting, mending,

reading for hours on end.
It's time to stoke the fires,
make soup and bread.

Time to dream of spring and warmth
and what we will produce next year.
We celebrate the snow and ice.

Siobhan Geraghty
Ottawa, Ontario, Canada
Hour 6

Strolling

i am soaked by chosen solitude
pebbles shake with each of my steps
delicate, displaced and dirty
they catch themselves in the soles of my shoes
as whistles of wild birds echo,
waning in the breeze
bruised branches
seemingly sleep at the side
as I rush to the lapping river

Megan Dobson
Austin, Texas, USA
Hour 11

unblinking

Witness this moment.

Don't look away.

Do not cheapen or discard the pain
the joy
the wonder
the fear.

See it all.

You don't have to understand,
but do not hide.

Honor it for how it will change you,
for what it can teach you,
and for what it cost.

Michellia Wilson
McKenzie, Tennessee, USA
Hour 1

THE TENDER SEASON

The light rolls in like thunder
on a night when crows rest
nervously on electric wires
just below the tree lines.

I look west - the direction of the sun plummeting into an envelope
of spring vegetation
and early darkness.

As expected, the trees are lined up
like soldiers beyond the clearing,
meeting this fresh spring sunset
in it's tendrils climbing toward sunshine.

The weather is already teasing us
with daytime warmth,
though the nights are painted on a cool,
sometimes damp tapestry.

Soon, the shoots, sparsely bursting
through gnarled limbs and brush,
will turn into leaves unfurling
in the tender spring sunshine.

Katrina Moinet
Llanfairpwll, United Kingdom
Hour 11

Bushcraft

I complimented my neighbour
on his bushy beard,
grown during these difficult times.
Unprecedented, in his lifetime.

I failed to mention my own full bush
left to thrive between my thighs.
By then we'd both donned our masks.
He mightn't catch my wicked grin behind the 3-ply.

He'd grown manly during these trying times –
kept his upper lip stiff, all by himself.
I'd let myself go and learned to accept.
Furlough ate my children's future wealth.

I wonder which small freedoms we'll choose
to exercise once prudence returns.
I fear the Brazilian variant
may crush my short-lived rebellion.

Memories

Nancy Ann Smith
Amherst, Ohio, USA
Hour 6

Getting There

Invited to run with daughter –
LOVE the daughter, Jenny May.
I admire her physical activity level –
she is 20-some years younger.

But, no, running is not comfy for me.
I prefer the pace at which I can see
the variety of weeds, trees, flowers, and
the breathing pattern does not change.

Let's notice these little white caps on clover.
Seems that when I was a girl, they were occasionally purple.
Be watchful of the three leaved vines on that tree;
poison ivy loves to climb on, and cling to, strong trees.

Did you know this orange jewel-weed is more than pretty?
It usually grows near poison ivy and really soothes the itch.
Oh, I wish I had known, when you kids were little –
this broadleaf plant has antiseptic elements for scrapes and such.

Your Bentley and Royce want to go faster, don't they?
They are accustomed to your energy level, and
they are fortunate four-legged brothers.
Perhaps – and most likely – you will take them for a real run later.

Look, here is a dandelion in its last phase.
You can make a wish and blow those seeds all around.
Papa Claude may have preferred all green grass,
but I just love the sparkles of yellow throughout my yard.

At this pace we can chat – how happy you are
with Amy's and Andre's baby news,
and how challenged you are with the team at work –
that resents your earnest efforts to supervise and maintain.
And we talk about getting back to God. He's waiting patiently.

So, thank you for this nice little jaunt at my grandmotherly speed.
Lots of grandmothers do run like you do –
traveling through the paths, seeing enough to stay safe.
But, I love our "chatting pace" and tiny nature study.

Anne Paterson
Calgary, Alberta, Canada
Hour 7

I Forgot

my mind is tired, fragile and sore.
the wheels don't grind and the axle froze.
my storage compartments, full of yesterdays, are locked, jammed, and
can't be seen today.
reminders, human and not, are what I rely on each day.
i'm sorry, what did you say?
i can't remember, I forgot.
words often struggle to spring forth,
misfiled in my storage bank, buried deep, in a pile of stuff.
where have you been?
what day is it?
where are we going?
i can't remember, i forgot.
i know your face but can't recall your name.
i know i know you, i think,
but where we met and how, i forgot.
my mind is so tired.
The wheels won't turn.
The axle is broken, fallen apart.

Karen B. Call
Aurora, Colorado, USA
Hour 8

The Older Sibling

As the older sibling, I was responsible for my sister.
My mother didn't tell me I was responsible, but as we walked
to school every day, just the two of us, I knew I was responsible.
When my sister fell out of the playground swing and hit her head
on the last day of school, I was responsible for taking care of her
and making her lunch when Mama worked. That summer we
stayed home, no days to the beach, because mama had to work
extra hours to pay for my sister's medical care. But then mama
took us to an aunt and uncle who lived near the mountains.
My sister and I had not met them before. Mama said she needed them
to help her take care of us so she could work more. She left us
with them but then I felt more responsible for my sister because they
didn't know us. They didn't know how my sister woke up crying
almost every night and how to help her stop. They didn't know
that all I really wanted was a quiet place so I could be alone and
read for a little while every day. If you have a choice, do not be
the older sibling. Be a younger sibling. Even if you know you
must listen to the older one boss you around, it will be easier
not to be responsible all the time.

Karen Mandell
Lynnfield, Massachusetts, USA
Hour 11

Lab Report

After school I took the stairs up to the third floor,
the chemistry lab, to finish the project.
The hall was empty this late
and I was the only student in the classroom.
I mixed what I had to mix, wrote down results.
The teacher came out of his small office
and watched as I soaped and rinsed
and placed the tubes on the drying rack.
I picked up my books, held them across my chest
as girls did and turned to say goodbye.
Wiping his hands with a rag, he said,
You're very sheltered, aren't you.
I had no idea what he was getting at.
I was a gabby girl but I had no words to answer.
Yes, I had watchful parents, my mother once
about to call the police because I didn't call
from my friend's house after school.
Was that what he meant?
What exactly did he want me to affirm?
I said goodbye sir and remembered
how much easier it is to walk downstairs than up.
But it wasn't only gravity that pulled me down.

Kristin Cleage
Atlanta, Georgia, USA
Hour 3

Pictures

In the olden days, when we all gathered,
parents, grandparents, children, grandchildren
bringing food to share. Laughing, talking,
taking pictures to remember the day.
Sometimes so many people taking pictures, we found
ourselves taking pictures of us taking
pictures.

Now, when I think back to those gatherings of
so many all over the house, crowded in the front
room, cousins piled on top of each other like
puppies, spread out in the other rooms,
I don't need a picture to remember. In
my mind's eye, I can see us laughing,
talking, eating and
snapping pictures.

Diane Carmony
La Quinta, California, USA
Hour 4

We shall see each other again*
(a poem in memory of Patti)

We shall see each other again, she said,
but don't come now.
The truth is, she said,
I don't want you to remember me this way:
frail and sad, slipping away.
Dying.
Instead, how about this?
How about you go to the ocean and
walk through the waves crying
while beautiful black shells wash up at your feet and
sea gulls scream into the winds
above you.
You can take carnations and fling them into the surf
and you can sing a song of your making
that will float
all the way from California to Indiana
to my waiting ears and
I will send you snowflakes and baby robins and oak leaves
and everything wonderful
that I can offer from my world
and you can send me
coyote songs and sun rises and mountains
and everything wonderful
from your world and
all these infinite joys will mix together
into a jeweled labyrinth
of our friendship and
then of course
one day
we shall see each other again
but not now, not now.
Just not now.

*title is from the last line of Peace is Every Step by Thich Nhat Hanh

Tamara Belko
Rocky River, Ohio, USA
Hour 5

Long Car Rides

They told me long car rides
were the most painful,
the time when silence stirs
sweet memories and tears surge,
those moments — raw, unavoidable grief moments.

They weren't wrong.
No,
those who suffered lose
before me,
were
not
wrong.

Two years
two years,
since my mother's passing,
and, mostly, I drive with the radio on,
the louder the music
the better to subvert silence,
loud music to prevent
the onslaught of tears,
that strike in the quiet, raw grief moments.

but sometimes

I chose the silence
I chose the silence
to remember,
to remember mom kneeling in damp earth,
tending to vegetables,
gathering clippings of yellow daffodils,
plucking ripe cherry tomatoes.

I choose silence
to remember mom nestled

191

beside her grandchildren, reading, singing…

I choose silence
to see mom kneading dough,
spreading her love through cooking
I choose silence
to listen for mom's voice, calling my name.
I must strain to hear...

Sometimes,

I just choose silence,
on the long car rides.

Choose tears to remember.

Oliver McKeithan
Milan, Pennsylvania, USA
Hour 7

Cinquain

Ocean's
Tranquil water
washes over my soul.
Cleanses memories of you, I
am free.

Ingrid Exner
Burlington, Ontario, Canada
Hour 1

In My Dreams

In my Dreams I Soar–
Phoenix-like I rise above,
buildings reaching toward
Sky dotted with clouds.
Delicate wings flap-
Lifting—Propelling—Soaring
through space.

Dreamy clouds dance
with me as I
Breathe freely—
for the very first time!
Clouds gently pass,
Space clears—
Openness appears!

I am Born Again
in this space
of Being!
Once cushioned by Clouds,
My Vision now cleared–
I stop—pause—inhale and,
Breathe that Breath,
long overdue!

Filled with Breath and Knowing,
I fly back down into
that clouded space
Holding onto–
Memories.

Kathleen Tighe
Sandpoint, Michigan, USA
Hour 12

Nonets of Grief

In her final moment I was there
as she was for me in my first.
I held her hand, prayed for peace;
one soft exhale, she left.
Life's lonelier now,
regrets remain,
Mom's love gone
with a
sigh.

I was miles away when my dad died
he was gone before I arrived.
We never said our goodbyes
nor talked of what matters.
I see him often
in dreams, on streets;
memories
linger
now.

My friend was struck with a brain tumor
and died during a pandemic
I could not meet with her then:
Visitors not allowed.
Again, no goodbyes,
no final words.
A good friend
there, now
gone.

To the young it seems that life is full
of promises, and hope, and love,
but time brings change, loss and grief.
The world grows ever small.
To live long one knows
the full extent
of loving
and its
pain.

JL Nash
Yorkeys Knob, Australia
Hour 14

THE TWO OF YOU

When I couldn't find the dog's leash
I called out to you and your sister
to return it to me.
You found it funny to lay it
outstretched on the floor
in clear view of where I had looked before.

You are never visible
when I lose what I need
but your laughter
filters across the portals.
Imagination is all I have
to conjure our magic days.

There's a silent peg on the line
where I caught a giggle
as you ran by me last Tuesday.
The two of you chasing the poor dog
for cuddles and pats.

There is no emptiness you fill
no remorse or regret aching
to be rewritten over Time's
false memories. There's just
you and me and this fancy
beyond wraiths and fairies.

I've not planned anything for tea,
but should I lose my left stocking
I'll be sure to call out and ask you
to check the dressing up box
in case you have mistaken it
just like you did before.

196

And tomorrow in the supermarket
as I pass the confectionary aisle
I'll hear you plead your very best
efforts to persuade me
and I'll laugh out loud
for the two of you.

Mary B. Smith
Peoria, Illinois, USA
Hour 11

Good Death

He had been sick for a while,
I followed his nurse, my instructor, inside,
my trepidation welling up.

A farmer, work showing in his calloused hands, lying in the middle of
the room,
A pristine hospital bed, in a small house.

His wife was there, reporting fading life.
The nurse encouraged her,
Tell him to go, that it is ok, he waits for you.

She whispers this to him,
And slowly, a tear comes down his face,
The last of his life sliding away, and it's ok.

Brittany Sabatino
Northern Virginia, USA
Hour 12

Sandpaper Love

I was not a slab of wood,
to cut down
and rebuild at will.

But yours was sandpaper love,
rough
where it should have been smooth.

Trying to improve me,
yet really remove me.
All the parts of me,
that didn't fit your blueprint.

I could never nail you down
to serious decisions.
And found myself shelved,
in favor of your desires.

I did not need a carpenter.
All you wood
ever see
were my flaws.

Mercies

Brittanei Wayne
Kansas City, Missouri, USA
Hour 9

This too shall pass

as the tidal waves across the shore of the beach
may depression fade
into tiny grains of sand
flowing from your hands
back into the sea
buried deep down in the abyss
drowning all of your fears
reemerging as a new person

Lily Marie Saint John Hawley
Portland, Oregon, USA
Hour 7

Mercy

Without fear
Allow pen to scratch along paper
Let pigment flow here

Without doubt
Allow creativity to spill out
And sweep you along the unexpected paths

Be gentle with the tender blooms of story
Hold gently the threads of narrative
Over which your imagination has power

Be merciful to the new ideas
And hold kindly to those which have long lingered
Awaiting their hour
And your attention

Stefanie Hutcheson
Lenoir, North Carolina, USA
Hour 9

Crumbs

That's the way the cookie crumbles—
bite by bite into pieces too small to eat.

Kind of like when forever ends
and the memories scatter in a flurry or haze.

The promises that bound them for eternity
turned into disbelief and unanswered questions.

But at one time that cookie was so sweet
The hardest choice was to linger or devour.

The thing about consumption though
is that once it's gone it's gone.

Better to savour those confections and not be so hasty
so that crumbs are not the only things that remain.

Renae Ogle
Phoenix, Arizona, USA
Hour 9

Don't Wait

Pain dulls the senses.

On overload, we shut down…
go into survival mode
allowing only the most basic needs
to have voice.

When this happens in succession…
when there is rapidfire negative stimuli,
this state becomes the new norm -
"this too shall pass" becomes
the new mantra.

our every day reality
our sense of joy and spontaneity
is on hold while we wait
for "this" to pass.

Don't Wait!

Join with the pain,
allow it to emerge
in tiny increments
from the fugue
our defense mechanisms
have mistakenly relegated it to.

This will, if done correctly,
safely move us out of
the waiting pattern
back to the NOW
which is actually the
only place there is.

Don't wait!

Mel McCarter
Hudson Valley, New York, USA
Hour 12

Child's Wisdom

Afraid, I walked with monsters.
I would become a wolf
loping through the night
showing fear my teeth.

Or, perched on a limb,
a bird before its first flight,
wings stretched, waiting
for a push. Then nothing

next taught me how to remember
the strength to survive. I had forgotten
until I saw a fawn struggle, weak

legs beneath it wobbling—
Frangible as a vase on the edge, it pushed
those legs into the ground and stood.

Britton Gildersleeve
Blacksburg, Virginia, USA
Hour 11

At the Storefront

The old man sat with feet propped up
gumboots scuffed through the black rubber
In his twisted fingers he held a needle
plying it through a patch spread over a torn net.
Overhead, a cloud pregnant with rain thickened
against the backdrop of a periwinkle sky.

This, he told me, *is how we always done it.*
The way my daddy done it. My mama
she brought him sourdough bread'n'butter
bread she made from her own starter
butter she beat from our own milk.
I miss them days. Nothing like 'em.

Denise Kolanovic
Massapequa, New York, USA
Hour 12

True Self

My true self is an angel
wrapped in joyous love.
I catch a glimpse of her
every now and then – she sings to me –
and kisses me when I cry.
She has carried me along many dark roads
when no one else was around.
In the mountains of monotony, she shines
her diamond light so I will find her.
But she never stays too long.
How I wish we were one again:
back before time defiled me and
life separated me into two selves.
So now I know who I really am and
who I strive to be.

Dane Lyn
Southern California, USA
Hour 1

shadows of rebirth

too many times, or perhaps not
enough times, I have crafted a new
veneer for this life, for my
persona, after all tomorrow is
another day, and another, and still
more. new beginnings collected in a firefly jar
of wishes to not be
me.

shadow upon faded shadow,
black and grey scars chronicling the
rises
and falls
of my gummed up gear filled phoenix.

Nandhini Natarajan
Rockville, Maryland, USA
Hour 11

My Friend Janey

Of fourteen children,
my friend Janey is the twelfth.
Seven older brothers tell her
where to go, what to do.
Janey says yes,
and does what she wants.

She tells me that in college,
I have to party.
Inexperienced, I completely agree.

Her brother Jerry,
the oldest, the strictest says,
Do not stay long.
Returning, do not use the deserted fields
as a shortcut.
Janey does both.
I plead and beg,
I have a healthy fear of Jerry.
He is elsewhere, she assures me,
At another party.

We cross the field,
I am sure we will be murdered.
if not in the fields,
definitely by her brother.

Suddenly Janey notices Jerry's car
On the road, around the fields.
Run, she urges.
We hike our sarees
And run.

210

Jerry stops where he can
intercept us,
and turns on the high beams.
We can be clearly seen,
but panic-stricken
we continue running
and laughing
hysterically.

The next day, Jerry shows
our friends
the pictures he took.
Fortunately,
all that is visible
are four skinny legs
and two sets of teeth
in the dark.

Farah Bagharib-Kaltz
Singapore
Hour 12

Walking On

How far is too far?
How late too late?
Is there room for redemption
as long as you're not dead?

Twenty-five years since your palm last met my face
Nineteen since you shoved me out the door
Not a day goes past when I don't think of you
and I do not want to anymore.

How do I forgive you
when you made me what I am?
Your motherless daughter, your childless child,
both of us, ewes without a lamb.

Twenty-five years since my palm found your face
Nineteen since I walked out that door
Not a day went past when I didn't lament you
But I will not lament you, evermore.

Carol Prost
Massachusetts, USA
Hour 16

Entangled

fat strutting chickens
contentedly clucking songs to self
room to roam, company of the clutch
sweet seeds, like heaven's manna, ever-present.

a simple peace, deep easy breaths
'til my gaze falls upon the broken body
little wild-bird trapped in netting
intended to keep the girls at home.

how long did you hang fluttering for freedom?
upside down, ruffled carcass, eyes now hollow.
if only I had heard your call, garden shears already
on the stoop, so easily I'd have set you free.

John Green
Bellingham, Washington, USA
Hour 5

He Soaks in a Tub of Hot Water

He soaks in a tub of hot water,
lavender essence, ginger root shavings,
a few drops of rosemary oil.

He closes his eyes, listening
to the soft music of Ravi Shankar –
sitar, a female voice, flute.

His mind wanders back to Thailand –
the monasteries, street food, people.
His heart broken, his savings spent,
his soul replenished.

Erin Lorandos
Phoenix, Arizona, USA
Hour 1

shadow position

in this case, the end
is a beginning

as the dance halls
fill again

partnerless feet
taking tentative steps

learning a new dance
called loneliness

but, she tells me,
at least we're here

survivors never dance alone

Cristy Watson
Calgary, Alberta, Canada
Hour 12

Ode to Signs

Cancer caused me to take stock of my
soul: discover what was missing –
gave myself permission to
dream in poetry. See
my life in stanzas –
rhyming couplets.
Lyrical
love of
words.

Ananya Panwar
Mumbai, India
Hour 11

What If?

How would things be
If
There was no rain?
Parched and cracked and dusty
Pleading for mercy
And all their tears, wasted and dry
Would fill not a babe's mouth
Not all their shrieks and suffering
All ribs splitting and cracking
And lips cracked and dreams
Cracked and shattered
Would burst open the clouds
Or bless them with mercy, with rain
And all the water flowing and wasting
Smelly and dirtied
Coloured and sullied
With leaves and flowers and corpses
With ash and bleeding starkness
All the waves raging and breaking
Will not grant a gentle wave
Of liquid water.

Denise Hill
Bay City, Michigan, USA
Hour 7

Normal is Welcome Here

"normal is boring"
the button on my backpack
announced to the world
as I coursed through my youth

spiked red hair
pierced eyebrow
and brooding countenance
confirmed

I wanted nothing to do with
status quo but to prod and dissect it
upend conformity
bend the will of approval

until an unseen force
turned the whole world
inside out
froze us all in a state
of desperation

normal was lost
a thing we didn't know we wanted
until we didn't have it
now suffer the thought
we will never have it again

that button is in a box
in the back of a closet
I dig it out and pin it on
to wear around the house

normal is boring
and I want it to know
it's welcome here

Amy Bostelman
Leander, Texas, USA
Hour 12

Pressed Blue

A pressed blue flower
Forever preserved summer
Generational Glory

Leila Tualla
Spring, Texas, USA
Hour 9

This Will Pass

This too shall pass, I think as another pain
shivers through me. I take another step, catching my
reflection out of the corner of my eye. *That is a walk
of a warrior,* I whisper. My legs have powered through so much.
My arms and shoulders have consoled the brokenhearted,
and carried the weak and dying.
This injury – a small hiccup –
this will pass.

Magic

Mary Eugene Peroja Flores
Quezon City, Philippines
Hour 5

Paradise

Once there was called a paradise,
the long stretches of ocean,
the breeze of gentle wind,
the steeps of a mountain,
after its knife-edge stone skin.

The trees and their variety,
where birds do sing and nest,
you'll be even more impressed,
To see what's out there in the west.

The fog in the atmosphere,
that being drag by the wind.
that chill-like feeling, as it touches my skin.
the trail of the mountain that leads you to the unknown.
until you saw something written, "Don't come back here anymore."

Danielle Martin
Trinidad and Tobago, West Indies
Hour 2

Coffee and Change

She awakens
in a fog
and though she tries
each time
in vain
her dreams wander off
leaving her alone
with wobbly thoughts
and daunting realizations
in this quicksand of shifting states

She seeks the magic
of a blackened brew
hazelnut, vanilla or mocha perhaps

Already she smiles
though it hasn't
touched her tongue
already
the magic has begun

Nykki Norlander
Sanborn, Minnesota, USA
Hour 2

The Joy of Unseen Things

the calm that spreads over you as you sit by the river;
steady, slow.
The love you feel in your heart when you look at a loved one;
warm, full.
The awe inside of you as you watch the stars;
amazed, transfixed.
The relaxation from hot cocoa or tea;
untense, silence.

Amanda Potter
Jacksonville, Florida, USA
Hour 15

Full vs. Half

The forbearance of leaving
my friends at the half
seemed logical

There's a new princess
due anytime now

the Poetess pondered

As her heart longed for words
long after midnight

that magical time

where headphones rock her
through, to the morning light

Alone

though not through her plight
those Word Temptresses
still sauntering by

Clasping my hand
saying "Come let's write!"

Halle Hund
Eden Prairie, Minnesota, USA
Hour 2

The Boat

Open air and closed eyes.
Soft breeze through hair
like a gentle lover.
Lapping waves and ocean spray cools
where sunlight beats down.
Smell of salt and algae;
anywhere else a sign of rot,
but here, freedom.

Jubilee Saint John Hawley
Medford, Oregon, USA
Hour 9

FLOW

What might happen
if you jumped
     the margins
          exceeded the lines
          let the ink
    twine
    along
    your
    fingers
    wind
    cursive lines
    up
    your
    spine
    flow
    with
    your
    blood
    circulate
    and
    stain
    your
    heart

What if
you made
visible
and
unblushing
your love affair
of words and sound

un bound
from the page
allowed
vibration
and
vibrancy
to find
F O R M
on the vessel
of voice
to
E
C
H
O
Have life
beyond
the ruled lines
and fragile seams
Alive
as poetry

Paul Sarvasy
Bellingham, Washington, USA
Hour 8

Photo Journey

The brick red soil at the edge
of my known world
has been prepared for planting
as two large gas balloons, rainbow colored
with an inviting festive aura,
hover, one above the other,
as border markers near the narrow basin
leading to the uncharted.
Squinting my eyes and looking
with a stubborn scrutiny,
the beyond merges with the low horizon
and will not yield to inspection.

I pack my knapsack with food,
bedding, water, a travel diary,
a camera, change of socks,
and search for a way
into the photo
to cross the tilled soil
so I can enter the hollow
and find a path
through it to that somewhere
just outside the limits
of my imagination.

Lexanne Leonard
Centennial, Colorado, USA
Hour 10

Spackle

One may think the color of water blue
ocean blue
but not rain

my drops are crystal
lucent

window spackle

magnifying
tiny bits
life you overlook

I remind you
notice small
tarry
there is much to see

Teresa Locascio
Santa Cruz, California, USA
Hour 4

Heartsong

it has always belonged to you
birthright, privilege, call it what you will
we are born into this world with something to claim
it echoes in the dark when one calls out your name
so often we are tamed, trained to ignore the draw
distracted by static, the manic crackle of all
of the outside world so loud it drowns out
the voice inside that says
that your magic is yours in whatever way it shows itself and
it has always belonged to you.

Jo Matsaeff
Brest, Brittany, France
Hour 2

About My Dog Lola

Lola was found in a cardboard box alongside her six siblings
on a countryside road one morning when she was a few weeks old.
A forest warden rescued the litter
and decided to raise them as his own.
Therefore, Lola never understood she was a dog.

Years after we adopted her, she'd still try and sit with us at the dinner table,
would ride shotgun in the car and sing like no one has ever sung
in the history of music.

Maybe she never was a dog. Whenever she'd feel either guilty or scared she
would start smiling, showing bright white teeth (usually scaring people away in
the process).

And just like other dogs she would also hate cats, love food and chase her ball
for hours. She was very jealous, funny and also a proud lesbian.

I think Lola was the first creature who showed me only you need to know who
you are. That it is okay not to have all the codes, to mistake a smile for a threat.
To growl at men. To be a human other humans don't recognise as such.
To sing your way through it all anyway.

Sangita Kalarickal
Minnesota, USA
Hour 8

A Process of Writing

Through the smooth keyboard,
my fingertips try to feel the letters.
I don't see the board, just the glowing monitor.
And the words merely appear.
Mute.
I cannot feel you, my words.
Do you know me?
I reach out to the ink pot.
A relic of the past, I fill up
the fountain pen,
And hear the letters coarsely
beckon as they appear
On my thick notebook paper.

Kevin J. O'Conner
Bellingham, Washington, USA
Hour 5

Time capsule

The time capsule is an old standby
in the popular imagination—
a hunt for buried treasure
a promise of revisiting innocence
an antidote to the popular complaint
Indeed, the time capsule
is an ever-evolving proposition
taking forms much different from what we imagine

And life is filled with repositories of time passed
from the lamp on the table to the bottle on the floor
framed pictures hanging on the wall
objects that produce sound, image
stories we keep on shelves

Yesterday I picked up a penny from the pavement

friendship

when days were long and i was saddened,
your kind sweet words were the best med.
just knowing you were near by,
brought a smile no tears.
friends for many years
are hard to find.
we are two,
it's true.
love

Alena Casey
Hawaii, USA
Hour 11

Violets

Cold snow withers
the violets we planted.
Frost edged purple
glistens, stems slanted,
beaten, beaten by wind.

Kneeling in mud,
by spring enchanted,
all's well and green
and fair as a lie.

I might have tried,
when blanch-white cold
rolled into my garden,
to save my violets
if you hadn't turned candid.

Christina Tang-Bernas
Anaheim, California, USA
Hour 10

Blue

the Blue of the ocean depths is
different than the expanse of
early morning spring sky
dusty sweetness of
fresh picked blueberries
delicate vein running beneath
the thin skin of my wrist
opalescent shimmer of abalone
wide eye of a peacock's tail
sheer pale deep of a glacier's heart
mottled violence of a healing bruise
yet all are Blue

Nasiha Sadhik
Puducherry, India
Hour 10

black

crow, crow, crow,
it's blacky black.
dark, dark, dark,
it's blacky black.
black is so, dark, is so hard, is so good,
not is so ugly and Worsley scared.
if it was scary, I never used.
if it was ugly, I never mind.
black is so sweet, is so cute, is so lovely,
it is a lovely colour.

Anshu Sikchi
Chicago, Illinois, USA
Hour 9

From the waters
I evolve.
And he drops
the jaws.

In the sunshine
I dissolve.
Yes, I am free
of flaws.

In the skies
I fly.
Up above.
I've also got claws!

A mystery
no one can solve.
I've grown against
Nature's laws.

Joyce L. Bugbee
Higganum, Connecticut, USA
Hour 11

Clouds of Happiness

Skyscrapers silhouette against the periwinkle sky
clouds spread softness
as bird wings beat the air
in an attempt
to flying in a cloud of happiness

Rhea Kumar
Palo Alto, California, USA
Hour 4

What's Above?

There is a flying thing in the sky.
Is it a bird? Is it a plane?
Could it be aliens?
Watching us from above,
not far but not close.
Studying us,
waiting for
us to
end.

Tina Blondino
Sammamish, Washington, USA
Hour 4

What Mask Do You Choose?

What kind of mask would you
choose for yourself?
For a mask holds magic, dreams,
power to take you beyond.

Yes, some masks hide,
pretend you are whole
when you're fractured,
at peace when you are jealous or angry.

But there are great powers of masks –
powers to open, to be more,
 to transform.

You can be the power of the sun –
 warm, enriching the earth.
You can be mountains –
ancient, tree-loving, slowly eroding.

You can be peace –
reach out, make clear,
 undiscouraged.
You can be poetry –
reveal truths below sight,
the workings of fate.

Now think –
what kind of mask
will you choose to wear?

Pamela Gerber
Southern California, USA
Hour 10

Connect the Dots

"Oh, don't even try to connect the dots,"
he said.
It's true.
The space inside and the one above
the cosmos of you and me,
no way to comprehend.
Particulate matter we are,
no less starburst than shredded skin,
chutes and ladders,
helix twist,
the cellular merry-go-round
that tells tales of why
you lie to me and I lie back.
We've grown accustomed to the fable.
New aliens and a nearby planetary commune,
where we respond in airwaves,
traveling to when the earth,
long gone up in flame,
reaches and touches
the vibrations they are.
He laughed when I said,
"Let's have a drink and test the vibe."
I meant it.
I, as matter, feel your integrity,
just as you feel my heat.
The light in me bows to the light in you.
A stuttering twinkling of time and we connect
the stars with fated fingers.
No body survives.

Meaning

Dan Tighe
Sandpoint, Michigan, USA
Hour 9

Island

I think I never saw anything else, I mean,
I only saw Islands,

Until I saw the sea.

(The dividing-definer of Islands:
does an Island exist w/o its definition?
Does a sound exist if no one hears a tree fall in the forest?)

… a 360-degree aquatic surround
and a certain geological dimension....

(Curtail the efforts to undo the importance of Islands,
as in,
No man is an island, and so on…)
Islands are important.

Islands require hard work to understand, I think,
(there's that insidious hurdle of the first person plural)
since
we are,
were,
always separate,
with a surround defining us, all that space between us,
us needing it to be otherwise, while it's not,
for this: *The bell tolls for thee* and so on....

Islands are important.

Without Islands, what use Love?

"No man is an island …" and "The bells toll for thee…" are quoted from John
Donne's poem "For Whom the Bell Tolls", taken from his "Devotions Upon
Emergent Occasions" written in 1624.

Jo Eckler
Austin, Texas, USA
Hour 10

Lost

Grief has its own gravity
Dripping down darkly
Achingly blue

Ngozi Andrew
Lagos, Nigeria
Hour 8

All Hot Air and Gas

If my life ain't altogether real,

at least I have the images in my head.

What is life if not a string of imageries?
a tapestry of slides real and imagined,
and a collation of what should have beens.
After all is said and undone,
sometimes we are left with but gas
and hot air to move us along.

Erin Rice
Greenup, Kentucky, USA
Hour 7

Normal
\'nȯr-məl\
adjective

1. the way i should have responded when you left. you said it so fast, i wasn't sure i heard correctly. i should have fought for you. asked you what i did wrong. after all, isn't that what society tells women to do? it always seems to be a woman's fault when the man leaves. when I was sure you were leaving, i should have cried. i should have written countless poems asking what i did wrong. isn't that what is expected during heartbreak? instead, i just stood on the porch and watched your taillights disappear in the rain.

2. how it felt when you left. i no longer felt like i was stuck in reverse. i could live my life on my own terms. "why is she so happy being alone?" i hear people whisper as i pass them. society tells us we should not be joyous in our independence. little do they know the truth of our relationship. i was finally free from my cage.

3. now, i lie next to him. i do not feel the need to watch my words. i do not feel the need to give more than i take. is this love?

Mitch Brown
Jacksonville, Florida, USA
Hour 12

No No Nonet

The written word speaks loud to the herd
Our attempts to entertain them
We speak and try, make them cry
Or give them hearty laughs
Attempts we have made
Some are a shade
A few words
Can mean
Much

Anne Farmer
Buckner, Missouri, USA
Hour 1

Keep Moving

When a shark stops swimming
it will drown and I realized sitting still
here in my own life, on this muted, sagging couch,
scrolling my phone, the television blaring,
I am gasping
for air beneath the choices I make.
Even happy that I am
Not tying my shoes,
or the morning air still swirls about without
me breathing it in,
the tree leaves sway solitary missing my
thoughtful gaze.
I settle further into that couch,
the stress of papers, piles, relationships
submerge me,
and carry me away from the light path
realistically still in my grasp.
Not even waving but drowning,
or clinging to a ray of hope
that might save me
but slowly, resignedly
dropping down, slumping still
the dangerous creature I am,
sinks to be with the other lifeless
beings below, paralyzed by inactivity,
thinking all the while
I should just
keep moving.

Tanya LaForce West
Muncie, Indiana, USA
Hour 2

Longing

distance surrounds her like water
cold, unyielding-smothering
where is she now
longing for the warmth
the warmth she used to know

winds blowing through and around her
cold, unyielding-relentless
where is she now
longing for the understanding
the understanding she used to be given

drowning, that's where she is
cold, unyielding-darkness
longing for the place
the place that seems lost to her now

Mildred Achoch
Nairobi, Kenya
Hour 19

Wonderfully Made

Am I a cliff
where what-ifs dive
into a sea of uncertainty?

Or am I a tumultuous sea
where my true self drowns
again and again

only to wash ashore
the deserted beach of self love?

Or am I a darkening sky
where the silver lining rusts,
where golden rays combust
Into the nothingness of apathy?

All I know
is that I'm fearfully
and wonderfully

Made.

Wendie Donabie
Muskoka, Canada
Hour 11

Reflection

As my kitchen window reflects my neighbour's home,
so, I see myself in you.
What I like and love about you, I like and love about myself.
What I judge about you, I judge about myself.

If I'm angered by your words or actions,
I'm angered by my own.
I see in you what I criticize in myself -
what makes me frustrated, frightened,
annoyed, sad.

You show me all of who I am;
my flaws and my beauty marks.

Recognizing our differences
and how we are the same
is how we learn acceptance,
how we come together.

To grow, to reconcile, to heal,
to build community, to become whole.

Farzana Suleman
Johannesburg, South Africa
Hour 6

You Got Me

When your ground is shaking
and your heart is breaking.
When you feel like you want to cry,
you don't even know the reason why.

I'll be there to hold your hand,
and support you when you can't stand.
I'll stay by your side
all day and night.

You can tell me all your secrets and lies.
I promise to keep them till I die.
I'll share your laughs, I'll share your heartache,
even in the moments when you break.

Through your dark times, I'll stick with you,
I will always stay true.
So don't be lonely, don't be scared,
just know I've always cared.

I got you and you got me,
together we'll have and incredible journey.

Stacey Graves
Marion, Wisconsin, USA
Hour 4

Invisibility

How much strength does it take to become invisible?

To blend into tacky wallpaper and stale conversation?

To be consumed by the deafening silence that seeps into every molecule,
every atom, the very nucleus of your existence?

How much energy does it take to scream into a crowded room where no
one looks up or bats an eye?

I saw Chicago and Mr. Cellophane became my anthem.

I wrapped myself in Reynold's wrap until I suffocated my own voice.

How much force do you need to generate to have someone walk right
through you?

You see, to me ghosts are merely memories, stuck on replay-

Over and over and over-

Trying to get it right.

To walk through me makes me a ghost.

Am I a memory? Am I stuck on repeat?

How hard do you need to push a needle to unskip a record?

I don't like the soundtrack of my life.

Fast forward-fast forward-fast forward,

Until it is all a blur,

Until I am invisible,

Until I am closed into your mind like a whisper, a dream that may have been a memory but now you've forgotten

Whether I am dream or reality.

Don't worry, I have the same problem all the time.

Kimberly Jay
Richmond, Virginia, USA
Hour 9

NOT FOR SALE

I am not for sale.

Not a toy for you to throw about

or stand on display whenever you deem it necessary.

I am not for sale.

The color of my skin is not a holiday you take when you want to experience life on the other side.

I am not a trip you take when you want to culture appropriate.

I am not for sale.

The trauma I have endured as a direct result of my melanin is not your story to be told.

I am not a book placed precariously upon a library shelf for you to browse about and peruse at your convenience.

I am not for sale.

I am not the angry black woman you've been warned about.

I am not the teacher, paid to answer your every question about what is appropriate and what is not.

I am not for sale.

And my voice is not yours to control.

Just in case you don't already know… the North won and slavery abolished, long ago.

I am not for sale.

Colleen Schwartz
Bellingham, Washington, USA
Hour 4

Dreamers and Prophets

"She dances back to the center of the room, its nexus of energy, feeling his gaze like a silk dupatta on her shoulders as she goes."

- From <u>Queen of Dreams</u> by Chitra Banerjee

I wear my disbelief
like a silk dupatta,
its gauzy fabric softening,
obscuring.

I wear my disbelief as I
dance to the center
of the room. Blues music
takes me down some
Delta road I have
never traveled.

This is the time of looking back.
And – also the time
to set my gaze on the distant land
of dreamers
and prophets.

This is the time
to remove my shimmering scarf,
my outermost layer.
Remove my separation from clarity.
And vision.

Cameron Chiovitti
Toronto, Ontario, Canada
Hour 1

When the Mental Illness Did Not Go Away

The day I graduated from the group home,
they took me off the Prozac.

Ingesting green capsules is not what made me better.
It was the knowledge

there are trees and birds and rapids just across the street,
and I am just as worthy as them.

It was the knowledge
my feet have a place to rest

when they've been bloodied by stones.
It was the knowledge

there are people in the world who cry
when my sadness screams.

The sadness learned to behave
in the presence of structure, but

this world does not provide structure
the way group homes do.

Maybe this is why I learned to seek out hospitals
the way others learn to seek out friends.

The world is a tricky place.
Its underbelly carries secrets

only those on the outside will understand.
I am trapped in its appendix.

(Why does the world have an appendix?)

I managed to infect the organ
with salty tears.

260

The surgeons had no choice but to extract me.
I was released into the world's lungs,

where I could learn to breathe
bronchioles of bounty.

I wouldn't say the world made a mockery of my breath the next day.
It was a gradual sharpening of the tongue.

It shaved my tastebuds
so I could not swallow the metal.

It severed my uvula
so I could no longer scream

for help.
Why did I even need help?

I believed I was fixed.
I believed I could make the world my own if I simply wanted it enough.

Maybe, I just didn't want it
enough.

Jennifer Faylor
Washington State, USA
Hour 12

Space

I never know about the spare units in me
until they become occupied.

I war with emptiness as if it were lack.
I paint it black, and try to reframe it as space.

A *no vacancy* sign shines out
my eyes, but it's a lie, there's room.

There's room for new hobbies,
room for love, room for things to learn.

There's room for new possibilities
while still leaving room for me.

L. Whitefeather
Tallahassee, Florida, USA
Hour 6

A Bridge

Your path is clear
Solid wood planks and rails
Stretch out before you
Bridging a deep chasm

Insects hum around you
Birds call soft warnings
A brook babbles far below
Your path is clear

You have a destination
Nothing to fear
An abundance of hope with
Solid wood planks and rail

Whispering softly
Flora surrounds you
Their leafy green shade
Stretch out before you

Just one sample
Of your life challenges
Trust yourself, and the way
Bridging a deep chasm

Sue Storts
Tulsa, Oklahoma, USA
Hour 12

The Urgency of Age

Ironic that we slow down
when there's so much left to do.
Nightmares of constant,
sluggish progress,
never reaching the destination.

Fear of dying before
the camel ride to Uluru.
Signs over New Zealand and Australia say,
"Closed for COVID. Try back next year."
Concern that the Chateau de Chenonceau,
even older than I,
will crumble before my visit.
Worry we'll miss sharing
that superb bottle of wine,
cellared for a special occasion.

Years are precious.
Patience wears thin
between holidays,
visits with family.

Kathy Pon
Central California, USA
Hour 11

Habits of a Curated Life

After Robert Hass's Habits of Paradise

Perhaps if I left the refrigerator door ajar
it would trend. Would I influence
wannabes, elicit elegance?
(My kitchen sparkles in morning light.)

If I captured the unwavering undertow,
moved waves of followers who yearn
for an ounce of sleekness, and if
this time I cared nothing for adulation,
power, elevated Instagrams, tossed stories,
would I still beam perfection your way?

A child opens her eyes to a world of
keyboards and grass, both smooth on skin.
Does it matter which pulls her closer
to herself? Identity is relative, not urgent.
Her smile, one post away from strategy.

Her mother is made of silver. Her mother
a social media zeitgeist.

Friends wait eagerly, eat her space & time.
She runs outside, leaves still life for later,
glazes a future with unforgettable moments.
What power, to woo with this magical touch.

Nishant Jain
Cupertino, California, USA
Hour 5

Iridescence

As the storm clouds gathered,
the trees turned to one another.
Bracing for the onslaught of wind and water,
they prepared for their tumultuous dance.

Everyone was well aware that
not all would remain standing.
But that was the way of the woods.

For those who made it through the night,
the sun promised nourishment and a glimpse.
Through the dark clouds it would gradually poke its hands,
till the rays met the sky in a dazzling ensemble of colors.
The light itself fractured into an arc.

As if to show the duality of nature,
the rainbow through its very existence,
seems to say,
that even from abject darkness can come great beauty.
It's all one and the same.

Richard Osler
Duncan, British Columbia, Canada
Hour 4

Time as It Turns

— After a Line by Guy Gavriel Kay

We must not imagine
we understand all there is to know
about the world. And what is what
he knows but a ripped page
thrown on a fire to become ash
and rise again as smoke before
it is gone for good? And knowing this
he wonders about the fawn that night. What
it thought it knew when first its mother,
and then that other, brother or sister, crossed over
and it stayed. Frozen. Now, on the other
side from its others. That fawn, immobilized and so
he kept driving on. Wheels turning. So much
turns and turns. The way of the earth, turning on its axis,
a thousand miles an hour. The way of wheels, turning, before
the leap. The fawn, released. Before the thud. The squeal
of rubber on a road.
And what does he know of the *why* of a god? The *if*
of a god? Or the no-way to stop
that fawn. Or a car, in time. Time as it turns.
     Or weeks before, no-way to stop
the young girl, needle marks
on her arm, from diving headfirst from high up
into the river. Not enough water
to keep her safe, unparalyzed.

Megan Dausch
New York, USA
Hour 10

More to This World

There is more to this world than the
problems we twist in our hands.
There is more to this world than the ache
to knit strands of confusion into a practical sweater.
There is more to this world than the full bowl of yesterday
and the untouched snow of tomorrow.

There is more to this world than the shining sea that polishes
the stones of our dreams.
There is more to this world than the endless sky.
There is more to this world than the stacks
of fears and hopes we never stop building.

There is more to this world than we can hold.
Yet together,
we hold the world.

Sabinah Adewole
United Kingdom
Hour 3

Ode to Freelancer

The bridge with views
The river overlooking the green
The woodlands on the river screen
The green on the walk offscreen

The Bridge with views
Photography her passion
Vacation her progression
The rock her disillusion

The Bridge with Views
Captures the scene distance
Gives in to her acceptance
The green every relevance

The trees with distinction
The views an illusion
The image an impression
The Bridge an experimentation

Rachel Durling
Talent, Oregon, USA
Hour 2

Unseen Joy

Today, someone made an anonymous donation that saved a life
or so I suppose, given the odds
Sometimes I think the only way we've made it this far
is because the world is seasoned with unseen joy
In a small Oregon town, a stranger wrote a letter to a prisoner
In a Himalayan valley, a flower bud could no longer contain it's craving
for the sun

Coins dropped again and again into empty coffee cups
from hands that wished they could do more
A toddler giggled at a spider crawling up her arm
Prayers were sent into space as the sun broke day around the earth
People danced in unison
People danced out of time
He learned to laugh at himself
She learned to say no
They forgave their mother before it was too late
Eyes timidly locked as the tunnel cut cell signal on the train
A newborn heard their first birdsong
The tide pulled away from a deserted beach
and a crab tapped a visual rhythm of footprints in the dampened sand

We capture snowflakes in high definition
permanently possessing their passing perfection
while spring births fawns drinking from snowmelt streams
high above the camera's gaze
in mountains that sound only of roving wild

It's that much more precious
That nobody ever sees the well of uncomplicated joy
behind my eyes
as I watch you sleep

Anjum Wasim Dar
Islamabad, Pakistan
Hour 2

Coffee and Change

Hot or cold,
I changed my drink,
my heart seemed to sink,
from tea to coffee, it made
me think–

Would it help to ease the pain?
to make me well again?
to bring good cheer to
the spirit and clear all
the strain of suffering?
I changed my drink.

Evelyn Elaine Smith
Waco, Texas, USA
Hour 12

Rejection

In Idaho, some twenty-years ago, I chanced upon a moldy, old high school beau,
a forest ranger in rubber gumboots with forty-something, middle-aged spread
(acknowledging old girl friends from more than a while ago engenders dread)
with yellow hair graying, and eyes no longer that exact shade
of periwinkle blue.
For time does cloud the vision of old flames,
for I'm surely likewise not the same.
His heart didn't skip a beat; he didn't hear me call his name and sounded retreat.

Solape Adeyemi
Ogun State, Nigeria
Hour 5

The Walls

Now that it's all said and done
Can we bring down these walls?
walls resentment and anger have built?
Can we bring down these walls?
walls paucity of communication and impatience have built?
Can we bring down these walls?
walls selfishness and lack of empathy have built?
can we bring down these walls?
Walls that riding roughshod over another's will have built?
Can we bring down these walls?
walls ethnic and tribal sentiments have built?
Can we bring down these walls?
walls religious sentiments have rigidly..built?
Can we bring down these walls?
walls self imposed by human thoughtlessness?
Can we bring down these walls?
walls that bloodshed and wanton blood letting have built?
Can we please bring down these walls?

Brian Dirk
Los Vegas, Nevada, USA
Hour 1

Story-Teller's Lament

Spend your life telling stories to folks,
and you start to believe a Lie.
That each story arc shall denouement,
before a character is allowed to Die.

I believed the myths we told ourselves:
used this to ignore every single sign.
And before I said what needed to be said,
the stroke cut out his mind.

You get one last conversation,
with everyone you know.
My last one with him I gave rejection,
and am now reaping what I sowed.

Marion Lougheed
Canada
Hour 5

Indian Burial Ground

The worst kind of time capsule is the one
you scurry to rebury
Bones you knew were there but
you hoped we would forget
Bones of brothers sisters children cousins and relations
Bones under the ground we walk, the grounds we celebrate

Cause of death unknown and yet–
Mothers fathers sisters brothers grandparents and elders know

They will not forget

Rebecca Resinski
Conway, Arkansas, USA
Hour 7

[She was]

She

was

a

garden

growing

quiet

disobedience

[an erasure from *The Grey Fairy Book* edited by Andrew Lang]

Shloka Shankar
Bangalore, India
Hour 11

How to Paint Joy

Drink a glass of sunshine.
Start with the brightest yellow you own.
Now harmonize it with your internal psyche.
Lighten it. Darken it. Repeat.
Flick your brush 'til you splatter the page with soul.
Make marks that whisper your name.
Highlight details and hang it up as a reminder

Jana O'Dell
Charleston, West Virginia, USA
Hour 8

My Truth

The breeze hits my hair as if it were calling my name
worried by my most recent choices–
I embrace the chaos, confusion and sadness that overwhelm me
trusting in my intuitive nature,
my ancestral calling to be by the sea.
Losing everyone in my life who doesn't understand,
doesn't take the time to even try–
Hoping to find the end of my story to be what we all hope it will be–
a happy ending.

Index of Poets

About Cynthia Hernandez

Cynthia Hernandez experiences life as poetry and expresses it through writing, photography, visual arts, and her relationships. Born and raised in Washington State, Cynthia has enjoyed a lifelong love affair with rain, sun, wind, trees, rivers, lakes, mountains, and the vast waters of the Puget Sound. When not writing, taking photos of birds, flowers or sunsets, or throwing herself into her work at King County government, Cynthia can be found in conversation, celebration and presence with her son Gabe, family, and friends. Cynthia has self-published two collections of poetry and is working on a third. She has thrice completed the full Poetry Marathon and looks forward to it each year. This was her first turn at editing the Poetry Marathon Anthology. More information about Cynthia's creative works can be found at www.barnesandnoble.com, www.amazon.com, and at www.palomacreates.com.